Get Out of That Dead-End Relationship *NOW!*

A Christian Woman's Guide on How to Get Real, Be Healed & Move On

Tonika M. Breeden

Get Out of That Dead-End Relationship *NOW!*

A Christian Woman's Guide on How to Get Real, Be Healed & Move On

Tonika M. Breeden

Get Out of that Dead-End Relationship NOW!
A Christian Woman's Guide On How To Get Real, Healed &
Move On

Printed in the United States of America, Durham, North
Carolina.

Breeden, Tonika Maria
Get Out of that Dead End Relationship NOW! / authored by
Tonika Maria Breeden

ISBN-13: 978-1500609740

Book Cover Design By: Bobby Barnhill

Editing Services by: Carla R. Cannon Enterprises, LLC

Initial Content Review by: LiyahAmore Publishing, LLC

Unless otherwise identified, Scripture quotations are taken
from the King James Version. Scripture quotations from
THE MESSAGE. Copyright © by Eugene H. Peterson 1993,
1994, 1995, 1996, 2000, 2001, 2002. Used by permission of
Tyndale House Publishers, Inc. Scripture quotations taken
from the New American Standard Bible®, Copyright © 1960,
1962, 1963, 1968, 1971, 1972, 1973,

DEDICATION

In memory of my father, the late Reverend Gerald Lamorice Tillman, I dedicate this book to you:

Dear Daddy,

I was in a dead-end relationship when you died.

I just wanted you to know that today, I am free.

Love,

Tonika

Table of Contents

Foreword by Carla R. Cannon

Get Out of That Dead End Relationship NOW! Is a must read for every woman who may find herself broken, battling insecurities, self-doubt, and low self-esteem as a result of previous unhealthy relationships. Author, Tonika M. Breeden shares her experiences within the pages of this book in an effort to show you that you too can come out of whatever bad situation you are in. Tonika provides hope to you as the reader that life is not over for you and no matter how low you may feel, Christ can raise you up again! Tonika serves as your one-on-one coach as she guides you on how to face and properly deal with issues for it is impossible to conquer what you are unwilling to confront. Tonika also shares wisdom from other authors in which she has researched in an effort to provide you with various ways to apply wisdom to your current situation. By no means does she convey that it takes a perfect woman to be found by a great man of God, but she teaches we are what we attract and it is time to get healed and become whole in order to attract God's best into our lives. To do so, we must first get real with ourselves in order to move on. This book is guaranteed to minister to the very depths of your soul. I have read it from cover to cover and as a single woman myself it has caused me to identify some areas in which I need to seek the Lord for healing as well. Therefore, no matter where you are in life whether you are currently in a great relationship now but perhaps still carry the scars and wounds of your past this book is a guaranteed source to get you from where you may be spiritually, emotionally or physically to where God ultimately desires you to be which is healed, whole and complete. I invite you to remove the mask and get ready to come out but first you must know it is possible and you deserve God's best. Greater is on its way to you now position and prepare yourself to receive it!

Carla R. Cannon
Publisher of the global, Christian publication, Women of Standard & National Best Selling Author of "The Power in Waiting" & "A Single Woman's Focus: Every Ruth Needs a Naomi". WWW.CARLACANNON.COM

Introduction: The Hole That Got Me Here

I had recently moved into my new house about one year after the divorce from my husband of ten years. I was now proud of the fact that as a single mom, I was able to purchase a home for my children. I was also grateful that I was stable and actively serving God in my local church. However, I distinctly remember coming home from service one afternoon with a strong sense of sadness and loneliness. As I began to reflect back, I noticed I would always sit in service and sing all the songs with great passion. I would smile and high five my neighbor to my left and right just as the pastor would instruct us to do. I can remember enjoying great conversations with my brothers and sisters in the Lord. I also served in the ministry and thoroughly enjoyed it. Afterward I would come home and lie down feeling sad and achy in my heart. I wondered what was wrong with me. I had an ache, a hole in my soul in which I didn't know what to do with nor how to heal it. I was doing everything right (or so I thought). I was taking care of my kids, had a great job, and was faithful at my local church to the point in which I actively served in other ministry activities outside of regular worship services. No matter what I did to feel fulfilled nothing could soothe my aching soul. Why was this happening? I thought I was healed. I thought I had it going on. From the outside looking in you would think I didn't have a care in this world. I had lost the baby weight I had gained from my last pregnancy and I looked good. But what was happening to me?

Ten years later, as I reflect back on my previous life, I can see clearly what that hole was, why it was there, and all the things I did wrong in an effort to fill and fix it. I now see how that hole drove me into situations and relationships that ultimately did not fill that hole, but rather caused it to grow. I also have come to realize the power of Christ in my life and to the point that no matter what anyone else will tell you, there is no man, church, ministry assignment, big-time career, amount of "looking good" on the outside that can fill the hole in our hearts other than the one who created our hearts and that is Jesus the Christ, the Son of the Living God.

In hindsight, I now realize that my dysfunctional relationship patterns began as a teenager when I did not know the love of Christ for myself. My early teenage romances were all based on infatuations and that initial high of falling in love for the very first time. I knew *of* Christ but I really did not *know* Him. I knew Him as my Savior, but I really had no clue about how to walk with Him in my daily life. All I knew was the pattern of the world and my emotions. I was not emotionally or spiritually mature. I did not know who I was. It took going through the pain of brokenness within relationships in order for me to really understand what Christ did for me and who I was as His Child.

It was during the process of being entangled in a dead-end relationship with a man who was an ordained minister which birthed this book. I did not seriously date until one year or so after my divorce was final and that was with a man who was not saved. Due to the great level of brokenness I was experiencing and my need for attention, I became involved with the first man who showed true interest in me and said all of the things I wanted to hear. However, I could not bear the thought of being involved again with someone who did not share my faith so I managed to end that relationship.

Not long afterward, I met the first Christian man who showed an interest in me. On top of that he happened to be a pastor. To make a long story short, I began dating him, fell in love and he began to share his desire to get married very early. Now of course this was what I always wanted – a Christ-centered marriage in which my husband and I could serve God together. He asked for my father for my hand in marriage. I began to plan our wedding and prayed for guidance on how to merge our blended families. In the midst of planning my wedding, my mom purchased my wedding gown. Due to his financial struggles, he could not afford to purchase an engagement ring therefore he gave me a ring which had belonged to his deceased wife with the promise that it was only temporary. I now look back on that and wonder how I could have accepted that.

Because I thought that we would be attending his church, I voluntarily left my own church to follow him. My church family at that time was not very responsive to the idea of me marrying him because they did not know him and neither did they have peace with the entire situation. I thought they were being difficult and didn't really try to understand or talk to us about it. This proved to make my life very painful.

Shortly after I left my church, he was basically forced to resign from his church within a few weeks. Now here I was without a church home and in a situation with a broken man who is no longer a pastor and without a real job. The marriage was put to the side in favor of survival and getting through the loss of not having a church and finding gainful employment. Throughout this time period, I was hurting and I saw the mess I was in but I still managed to have faith and hope that things would turn around for the best and that we would pick things back up regarding the wedding. Long story short, we both admitted that we did things prematurely and we were not ready.

Living like this year after year -- not really spending time with him, giving up so much of my time and resources to help him rebuild his life, never spending any holidays together, exchanging Christmas gifts in the parking lot, wearing the promise ring, family and friends forever asking questions which eventually wore me out. Over time, there were too many gaps, lies, inconsistencies, canceling dates, failing to show up when he said he would and just an overall lack of integrity. The gap between what his words said and what he actually did began to increase drastically. Not only that but I began to see clear evidence of other women. There was always the niggling sense that there was a side of his life that he deliberately kept away from me.

Once my father passed away suddenly, the whole situation in conjunction with the grief began to become completely unbearable until one day I gave him the ring back. Once I lost my father, I realized I could not keep wasting my time like this by putting my life on hold for a man who clearly had no intention on marrying me. Six months from the time I gave him the ring back, I officially ended the relationship. During the six month time period my eyes began to be opened to a lot of things and his behavior became even worse.

Shortly after the break-up, I sat down with tears streaming down my face and wrote each of the chapter headings as my personal confession. I originally named these confessions as *"Laws"* and entitled the piece as *"Relationship Laws for Ladies Who Love God."* I then published it to my blog and sent it to an online women's magazine where it was published there as well. It was instantly the most viewed page during that month. I knew then these confessions, lessons, or laws had resonated with thousands of women and I had to write this book.

Each chapter represents a lesson I learned during this relationship that finally gave me the courage to end it. Throughout the relationship, I would continually pray: *"God take this mess and give me a message. Take this test and give me a testimony. Take my scars and make stars."* This book is the sum total of the message, testimony, and the stars He has given me to help bring deliverance and freedom to other godly women who are broken, stuck, confused, and hurting in a relationship that is going absolutely nowhere.

My desire is to help other women not make the same mistake I did which was to assume that just because a man is a Christian or has a title in the church that he is *"The One"*. The major factor that kept me in this relationship much longer than I should have is the simple reason that I made it an issue of faith by truly believing that he was my God-ordained husband in spite of the very clear and strong signs that he was not.

In writing this book my goal is to help Christian women walk in wisdom and to avoid self-deception regardless of a man's title, position or even what he *says* about his faith walk with God. I had to learn that you must know a man by his fruit. You know who he is by how words line up with his actions.

This book is divided into lessons I've learned throughout my journey in three distinct stages. First, I had to get real and face the truth about myself. Secondly, I had to go through an internal healing process. Lastly, once I was healed and strong enough, I was able to end the relationship and move on. Within each stage, I share the lessons learned along with reflective questions, scriptures and quotes by various authors.

Part One: Get Real -- The Underlying Issues that Attract Dead-End Relationships

Chapter 1
Having a Faulty Foundation

Becoming Rooted, Grounded, Fixed & Founded in the Love of God First

One of the most important issues that contributed to my poor relationship choices was my lack of a true foundation in Christ. I was not rooted or grounded in the love of God. I knew God loved me, but I really didn't have a real solid sense or knowing of His love for me in a tangible way. Because of this, I was vulnerable to worldly concepts of what love is and did not have a deep foundation in God -- just the very shallow one established as a child in a Christian home. I was rooted in my own sense of self, the opinions of others and worldly things. I had to learn what it really meant to be rooted, grounded, fixed and founded in the love of God for myself.

To be rooted in the love of God means to have the depths of your being attached to Him -- not to another flawed human being, a material object, or any other thing on this earth, tangible or intangible. This includes money, status, titles, jobs, and other people's opinions. The word *"grounded"* is defined as being close to the ground or low. To be grounded does not mean that you think "low" of yourself in the negative sense of the word. Neither does it mean that you are to keep yourself in a "low status" in which you never aspire to do great things with your life.

What it does mean is that you have roots that go deep in God. It means that your soul is submitted to God and is not puffed up against Him. Being grounded under the mighty hand of God is another way of being surrendered as an act of your will under Him. God uses various circumstances and situations to keep us "grounded" so that we do not get too high and puffed up. From a spiritual perspective, becoming high-minded means to develop a haughty or prideful spirit because of our gifts and abilities. When we are grounded, we are dependent upon Him. We are stable and settled. Should we get too high without Him, we lose our footing, becoming unstable and vulnerable. To be grounded in the love of God also means that you have humbled yourself before Him and are not highly exalting yourself and your ways of doing things.

"Fixed" is defined as being firmly in position, stationary, and not subject to change or variation. When we are fixed in the love of God, we are in our proper position as children of God. We do not come down from our place of dignity and security as His daughters to chase or struggle to be loved. When we are fixed in anything (a man, titles, money, and other worldly desires) instead of Him, we are out of place, subject to constant changes, and forever fluctuating. Christ is not like that. He is not up and down or all over the place. We can count on Him to be the same as Paul writes in Hebrews 13:8 (KJV), *"Jesus Christ is the same yesterday and today and forever.* If He lives in us fully, then we should be stable just like He is. We are also admonished in 1 Corinthians 15:58 (KJV) to be *"stedfast, unmovable, always abounding in the work of the Lord."* As women of God who are rooted, grounded, and fixed in Him, we are to grow more steady, stable and settled as we mature in Him.

When you are rooted, grounded, and fixed in the love of God, fear is removed from your life. Where fear exists, love is not perfected or matured. According to 1 John 4:18 (NET), *"There is no fear in love. Perfect love drives out fear, because fear has to do with punishment. The one who fears is not made perfect in love."* If you are un-rooted, ungrounded, moving, and variable then it stands to reason that there is a lot of fear operating in your life. Fears such as the fear of what people think, the fear of not having a man, the fear of not having enough, the fear of being embarrassed, and the fear of making mistakes. This type of fear brings torment because you are rooted in something or someone else other than God and you will inevitably be let down.

However, if a woman is rooted, grounded, fixed and founded in the love of God for herself personally, she no longer has a reason to walk around afraid. She no longer makes fear-based decisions in an effort to control outcomes or manipulate others. She makes faith-based decisions for her life rooted in her deep knowledge of the love that God has for her.

A foundation can be defined as the basis on which a thing is founded or supported. It is the act of founding or establishing the basis or groundwork of anything. Your life must be founded upon Jesus Christ Himself, the Chief Cornerstone. A building cannot stand with a faulty foundation. If we are not founded in Him, we cannot expect the structure of our lives to stand. In civil engineering, there is a concept known as structural integrity. Buildings, roads, bridges and other large public facilities must pass tests to ensure that their structures have sound designs with the highest level of safety standards, workability, and capacity to withstand catastrophic events. If a building lacks structural integrity, it does not pass the test. The same goes for our lives. If we refuse to build the foundation of our lives upon Christ and choose our own weak building materials, we lack structural integrity. When the storms of life and temptations come, we will fall apart.

Building your foundation takes time. No solid building that has structural integrity has ever been quickly thrown together in a sloppy manner. Things that are built to last and endure storms must be built correctly. Taking shortcuts -- the easy way out or the fast way to get what we want or where we think we need to go can wreak havoc later on. We must learn to wait on God and work with Him in order to build our lives as He sees fit and in His timing. When we bulldoze ahead in our own power, we make a bigger mess of our lives. When building our lives, "God takes the time to do everything right – everything. Those who wait around for him are the lucky ones" Isaiah 30:18 (MSG). Without waiting on Christ to build the proper foundation and structure for our lives, we will create our own insecure and unstable foundations based on emotions, fears and desires.

Deep-seated and unresolved insecurity is what causes a faulty foundation. A young woman without a fundamental knowledge of who she is in Christ and her worth as a child of God can easily get caught up in the romance and drama of relationships, beginning in her teenage years and once that first relationships fails, she will continually seek that initial romantic high of that first infatuation. She has no clue about who she is in God and is only driven by emotions and flesh. We can be mature spiritually as women of God, but still emotionally immature because we are stuck at the same age emotionally from that first time we fell in love. Some of us are well into our thirties and forties and are still looking for that same romantic high that we received when we were 16 years old. We have not allowed God to heal and grow us up emotionally. We are stuck.

This marks the beginning of relationship insecurity, romantic addiction, or anxious love in a woman. This can drive and play a huge role in all of her relationships with men going forward. Society and media continually paint the idealistic picture of romantic love instead of true, mature, agape love - which is what marriage and true love really is all about -- Christ's love for the church as His bride. We look to our husbands, boyfriends, fiancés, and significant others to meet our deepest emotional needs. We forget that these men are human and frail, prone to weakness, and sinful as we are. We put all of our fragile, emotional eggs in one man's basket, only to discover that there are holes in the basket when the eggs start sliding out and breaking on the ground. The poor man simply does not have the spiritual, emotional, and physical capacity to handle all of our needs.

God knows we need human companionship; after all, He created the institution of marriage. Women need men and men need women. But we can't look to a man to meet *everything*. There is a place in our hearts that only our Creator (not our man) can fill. We have these grand expectations of high romance, deep conversations, and tenderness then look at our man and realize that he can't deliver on that level every day. We then unravel and become emotionally unglued. We quickly find that we were rooted, grounded, fixed, and founded in our fantasy idea of romance instead of God. I cannot tell you the countless times I have spent fantasizing about my ideal relationship on only to see my man act the total opposite and then I would be a hot mess! You know you have done this too!

It is better to rely on God for our emotional needs and all other needs, seeing as how He knows our frame, our thoughts, the "why behind the what" on every weakness, strength, thought, plan, dream, struggle, and behavior we have. He knows it all anyway. God loves us in such a deep, holy, profound way. His love is perfect. He knows us on a cellular level, i.e. He knows every cell of your body before conception and each hair of your head has an assigned number (Matthew 10:30 KJV). No one on the face of the earth occupies your particular place in time and space with the same particular combination of thoughts, behaviors, gifts, talents, and life experience. You are a fearfully and wonderfully made one-of-a-kind woman. God knows this better than we do, yet we still trot around looking to our man and others instead of looking to Him our Creator.

What Does Being Rooted, Grounded, Fixed & Founded in the Love of God Look Like?

When a woman is rooted, grounded, fixed, and founded in the love of God, she is at peace within and without. She carries a quiet confidence and radiance about herself whether she is single, divorced, or married. She has learned to love and accept herself for who she is in spite of her flaws, weaknesses, and shortcomings. She has become comfortable in who she is, period. Her confidence in the God living within her and loving her keeps her totally and completely secure. She is not dependent upon outside props, situations, material things, or positive circumstances to make her feel good about herself. She is at rest in the love of God for her. She has finally learned how to receive, walk in, and live in the love of God for herself without struggling, huffing, and puffing for a man or anyone else for that matter to love her.

She is able to love herself; therefore someone else can love her. The greater the revelation of the love of God that a woman has for herself personally, the better she is able to love herself and someone else. She sees herself as God sees her: fearfully and wonderfully made, a daughter of the King, and a child of the Most High.

Because she knows who she is in Christ, she has no need to compare, compete, or contend with anyone about anything. She does not compare herself to others because she realizes that everyone is in different seasons of life, at different levels of maturity, with different backgrounds and lives than she has. She has no need to compete for a man, money, or any other resource for she knows that God is the source of all creative power. She knows that she can simply declare the Word and the creative force and power of the Word of God will bring into fruition that which she desires in God's timing, way, and will. She simply holds her peace and let's God fight her battles.

From this place of being rooted, grounded, fixed, and founded in the love of God, she is now in a position to make quality decisions with discernment regarding her relationships. Because she is not desperate and needy for attention, chasing and searching for a man, or working herself to death for praise and pats on the back from others; she can simply do whatever God places on her heart to do with grace and excellence.

She can be trusted with higher levels of assignments, prosperity, leadership, and other blessings because she has the emotional, mental, and spiritual capacity to receive and retain such blessings. She is not operating at an emotional or spiritual deficit where she would be using these things to fill voids that only God can fill. She is already full and not lacking. Thus she serves from a place of wholeness not brokenness.

She has wisdom to carefully guard her heart and not give it away to the first man who makes the right noises or says the words. She has the wisdom to guard her heart in all relationships because she rightly judges by fruit, not words. She takes her time before she opens the door to the intimate places of her heart and life to just anyone. She takes the time to know someone in all four seasons of the year before she commits to anything financial, relational or in business. She operates in wisdom in all of her affairs.

Reflect on God's Word

1. 1 Corinthians 3: 11 (NET*) "For no one can lay any foundation other than the one already laid, which is Jesus Christ."*

2. Isaiah 28:16 (NIV*) "So this is what the Sovereign LORD says: "See, I lay a stone in Zion, a tested stone, a precious cornerstone for a sure foundation; the one who relies on it will never be stricken with panic."*

3. Ephesians2:20 (NLT) *"Together, we are his house, built on the foundation of the apostles and the prophets. And the cornerstone is Christ Jesus himself."*

Things to Think About:

1. Reflect upon your relationship history, beginning with the first time you fell in love. Are you easily infatuated? As a grown woman, after you have been dating someone for a while, and the excitement cools off, do you find yourself forever trying to find a way to get the relationship back to the initial first excitement? Are you in love with the idea of being in love? Real, true lasting love comes from being filled from within with the love of God for yourself and not relying on another individual fill you up. Once your love tank is filled with the love of God, you will no longer struggle emotionally when the excitement dies down in your romantic relationship. Continually work on filling your own love tank by meditating on His love for you!

2. Jesus is the Cornerstone. He is of prime importance. He is the first stone in the creation of your life to mark the construction and re-building of a new you. Once Jesus is established as your Cornerstone, then you can build a structurally sound life foundation. Reflect on the scriptures above and examine your life. Is Jesus Christ the Cornerstone of the foundation of your life? What is your identity as a woman founded upon?

3. Are there areas in your life where you did not put into practice godly counsel and wisdom and suffered the consequences? Don't be foolish. Take the time; count the cost to build a sure and stable foundation of your life with Jesus as the Cornerstone and the foundation.

Chapter 2
Not Being Complete In Christ

What It Really Means to Be Complete In Christ

I can distinctly recall the first year or so after my divorce. I did not realize how emotionally broken and needy I was. I found myself falling for the first man who showed sincere interest and that told me all the sweet things I so desperately wanted and even felt I needed to hear. I was starved for attention that I never really received from my husband in my marriage. At that time, I was able to overlook over the fact that the first man I dated was not saved and did not see any reason to attend church. He told me I would be a good wife and that I was a beautiful woman. I was fresh out of a divorce from being unequally yoked for almost 10 years and here I was again getting myself emotionally entangled with the another unsaved man who happened to be a bit nicer and more tolerable, but nonetheless totally not interested in the things of God. I later managed to end this relationship, but because the void was still there, I found myself yet again entangled in another relationship - this time with the minister who also proved to be another dead-end. I know what you are thinking. I can hear you saying, *"Tonika girl, get it together!"* But the truth of the matter is that I was to the point of desperation to be touched, loved and cared for that I would do anything to ease the pain I was feeling.

Why did I get so easily entangled again? It was because I was not complete in Christ. I did not need an unsaved man to tell me I would make a good wife or that I was beautiful because these things were already true. But in my mentality and low state during that time, I needed to hear that from the outside instead of from Christ within. I had an inner cry that said *"See Me-Hear Me-Notice Me-Love Me"* that was never satisfied and that could never be satisfied with mere flawed human. I had to learn the hard way that this an inside job where I had to allow Christ to bring completeness in every area of my life from the inside out. This is the sum total of completeness.

To be complete in Christ is a very interesting and somewhat challenging statement to comprehend, yet here it is in the scripture where Paul wrote in Colossians 2:10 (NKJV) that we are complete in Jesus Christ. Completeness is another word for wholeness. You cannot be whole and yet be incomplete. You cannot be complete, yet lack wholeness. We receive this completeness and wholeness when we receive and accept Christ.

To be complete in Christ means that once you have received Him as your Lord and personal Savior, you have been placed in right standing with God. At this point, you are not missing or lacking anything necessary for abundant life and godliness. We can also take a look at the root meaning of the Hebrew word *shalom*, which is generally translated as peace and is found throughout the Old Testament. The deeper meaning of this word according to Strong's Concordance 7965 is completeness, wholeness, health, peace, welfare, safety, soundness, fullness, harmony and also the absence of agitation or discord.

It is entirely possible for a woman to receive Christ, yet fail to walk in completeness, wholeness or shalom. Many of us as Christian women are truly saved and love the Lord, yet we continue to operate with an emotional and spiritual deficit. This deficit spills over into other areas of our lives including our health, finances and relationships. Although Christ died for us to become complete in Him, we must deliberately choose to walk in that completeness every day. These types of choices are the ones in which we choose to fill that soul deficiency with the love of God through His Word, through sound godly counsel, praise, worship and fellowship with other believers. These are the choices that facilitate spiritual and emotional health, godly self-esteem and internal strength.

Even if we are saved, we are at our most vulnerable when we have just endured some type of loss, grief, or hardship. It is during these times that we question our value. We feel the need to be pumped up from other people in order to feel complete. We need to be fortified and strengthened from outside of ourselves because we lack the fortitude that comes from Christ within.

What caused me to have trouble in my relationships when I chose to look outside of myself, specifically to a man to complete me? It t is "not good for man to be alone" however God brought the helpmeet to the man (named Adam) who quickly identified his helpmeet. Adam did not hesitate to make the determination that Eve was *"The One."* Eve simply showed up on the scene in all of her loveliness, fully complete and whole in God. She did not look to Adam to complete her. She did not need Adam to say that she was a "good thing" because she already knew it. She did not look to him for validation that she was his wife.

The Need to Be Married to Feel Complete

Because I wanted to be married, I had a deep need to be validated as a wife or a true helpmeet. I read everything I could find on biblical marriage and how to be a godly wife in an effort to not only be ready for marriage when it occurred, but also with the underlying motive of being seen as wife material so that the man I was with would go ahead and marry me. I tried to implement everything I learned in the books I'd read within my dead-end relationship in order to show him that I was *"The One"*. My attempt to do this did not work because my motives were wrong. All it did was gave him access to my life as I attempted to treat him like my husband when he was truly far from it!

While operating out of a broken, unsound, and agitated state, I found myself settling for less because of my need to be validated. I learned the hard way that if I have to huff, puff, jump through hoops, and sweat to show him that I was his "good thing" , then I was not the one for him and neither was he the one for me. My huffing and puffing involved reading and studying over the books, praying, hoping, crying and over-giving of myself so that he would see how much I cared and what a wonderful wife I would be to him. You see, I was too busy trying to prove myself rather than simply being who I was. When you are broken and wounded you will do things you normally would not do.

The need for validation as worthy wife material in order to feel complete as a woman comes also into play when our biological clocks start ticking. Sometimes that biological clock is ticking like a bomb so loud that it is the only thing we can hear! We also do not feel complete as a woman when we are lonely and desire companionship. We become agitated and lose our peace that Jesus died for us to have. Functioning from a position of quiet desperation and anxiety will actually repel the man that God has for you. The man God has for you will show up and identify you as "the one" or his "good thing" when you exhibit the poise and grace that comes from being complete and whole in Christ.

The one God really has for you will not need for you to prove anything. He will already know the caliber of woman you are and will value you. He will not waste your time. However, being broken and incomplete as a woman will cause you to overstay your welcome in an expired relationship because you are still trying to prove that you are "the one" he should marry. You will hang on believing for the best when he has already moved on. This is exactly what I did. I overstayed my welcome in a relationship that really should have ended within the first year, but because of all of the things he said and did in the beginning of the relationship that indicated he was serious about marrying me, I lingered on in the hopes that things would turn around. Sister, it is like keeping an expired milk jug in the refrigerator thinking that the milk is still okay because it doesn't smell bad. Throw that expired stuff out now!

The fact that you are a fearfully and wonderfully made child of God is enough validation by itself! No longer seek validation from others and refrain from searching outside of yourself when all that you need resides within. You already have all you need to be whole, healed and free. Embrace it and accept it as your truth. You need no further validation from anyone.

Reflect on God's Word

1. Psalm 139:14: *"I will praise You, for I am fearfully and wonderfully made; Marvelous are Your works, And that my soul knows very well (NKJV)."*

2. Colossians 3:10 *"And you are complete in Him, who is the head of all principality and power (NKJV); and in Christ you have been brought to fullness. He is the head over every power and authority (NIV)."*

3. Ephesians 1:6 *"to the praise of the glory of His grace, wherein He hath made us accepted in the Beloved. (KJV)"*

4. 1 Peter 5:10 (AMP) *"And after you have suffered a little while, the God of all grace [Who imparts all blessing and favor], Who has called you to His [own] eternal glory in Christ Jesus, will Himself complete and make you what you ought to be, establish and ground you securely, and strengthen, and settle you."*

Things to Think About

1.   As shown in the above scriptures, once you have accepted Christ as your Savior, you are already complete in Him. It now becomes a matter of living it out in your daily walk. It becomes a matter of moving beyond salvation and entering into the deliverance process of becoming complete, whole and free in your mind and soul. Ask God to show you the areas where you are still functioning at an emotional or spiritual deficit. These would be

the areas of brokenness or wounds that are still yet unhealed in your life. As Best-Selling Author of the book, *Black Women Redefined*, Sophia Nelson states, *"You can't fix what you won't face."*

2.   Can you identify instances, relationships, issues or things which you have reached out to for completeness or validation of who you are as an individual? What was the result?

3.   Have you ever worked to prove to a man that you were "The One" for him and in return it did not work the way you intended? How has this led to further brokenness? What will you do differently? During this season of your life, take the necessary time for you to heal and be completely you; who Christ made you to be.

Chapter 3
Boundary Busting Behavior

Personal boundaries are "guidelines, rules, or limits that a person creates to identify for themselves what are reasonable, safe and permissible ways for other people to behave around him or her and how he or she will respond when someone steps outside those limits." It is like your own personal "line in the sand" that distinguishes you, your world, and values from everyone else. Boundaries define the limits and parameters in which the people in your life must function in order to have healthy, mutually satisfying relations with you.

It takes serious soul-searching, quiet time, and a healthy dose of self-respect in order to know who you are, what you value, and what you will or will not tolerate in your life. Most of the time, we do not take the time to do this until we have been heartbroken or gone around the same old mountain a few times before we finally get it. If you do not take the time to dig deep and look into your life – what you stand for, what you value, what is meaningful to you, what brings you joy and peace and what steals your joy and peace -- then it will be very difficult for you to establish any boundaries. When you know who you are and whose you are it becomes much easier to (1) know your boundaries and (2) enforce your boundaries. This is a growth process in self-confidence. It is one thing to grow to the point to know what you will or will not tolerate in a relationship, but it is another thing altogether to enforce it in the heat of the moment when things are happening in a relationship.

Boundaries in relationships help you to know when someone has crossed the line in their behavior towards you. When a person steps to you incorrectly or asks you to do something you know is absolutely out of line, it should be your warning bell; a "ding-ding-ding" should go off in your mind right way. This is your *boundary line* working. The problem with most women is that we love to give the "benefit of the doubt" or we convince ourselves that "it (the behavior in question) was innocent and we misunderstood or overreacted." We question and second-guess ourselves when our boundaries start "dinging," and then later wonder why things went down the way that they did. The reason why we do this is because we want so badly to please others. We want to be validated. We don't want to hurt the other person's feelings. We don't want them to think "bad" of us. The reality is that this person obviously doesn't really care about your boundary or else they would not have tried to violate it in the first place. Or could it be you were not clear on what your boundaries were? We often bust our own boundaries in the name of love in order to please a man. Writing from her personal experience, Mandy Hale of the book, *The Single Woman* states:

"…But I didn't do that. I felt bad, guilty even, for putting him in an awkward position, when clearly he couldn't have cared less about the position he was putting me in… Bottom line I was taking on the establishment of a boundary that he, as the pursuing man, should have taken on. And I put my own feelings of hesitation aside to keep from "hurting his feelings" or making him think I was "rude" or "mean." I say all this to say…SET BOUNDARIES, with your heart, your time, your LIFE. Not everyone who knocks on the door of your life should be allowed in. Not everyone has good intentions. This is not to say you should barricade your heart behind a brick wall and never allow anyone in…but you do owe it to yourself to protect yourself. You shouldn't be the one doing all the bending, and the stretching, and the compromising. People who truly want to be in your life and belong in your life will ALWAYS be willing to meet you halfway. And if they're not willing to meet you halfway, perhaps they shouldn't be given the pleasure of meeting you at all. So cultivate discernment, take your time, get to know people, and only THEN welcome them into your life. Trust is to be earned, not just handed out freely. Boundaries will only ever offend people who aren't really all that invested to begin with. And anyone who

wants and deserves to be in your life will always respect your boundaries, period. End of sentence."

Speaking from my own experience, there are two distinct areas where I did not have strong enough boundaries because my identity was tied up in becoming a wife instead of becoming the full and complete woman God created me to be. I compromised myself in the area of sexuality and also in terms of over-giving of my time, talent and resources to a man by treating him as my husband, when in reality he was nowhere close to functioning as a fully committed man, much less a husband.

Boundaries in Sex

In the relationship with the minister, I had a sincere desire to do what was right in the sight of God. Eventually, I did give in to his demand for sex outside of marriage within that first six months, but I simply could not handle the guilt of what I had done. When I took a stand for righteousness and told him that it would not happen again, he seemed to agree but eventually became intimate with someone else. In hindsight, I now can see that although he had a calling on his life, remaining abstinent was a joke to him. He simply moved on with other women who were willing, but in my naiveté, I wanted to believe the best. I wanted to believe that he was faithful, but eventually I had to wake up and smell the coffee. He kept me around to assist him with his business initiatives and to boost his ego. Because I loved him, I did not want to give up on the relationship so easily. I did not enforce my boundaries to say that this behavior was unacceptable and simply end the relationship. What in the world was I thinking? I must have bumped my head to continue in this relationship knowing that he was sleeping around!

Any man who claims to be a true child of God will want to protect the purity of the woman he claims to love as Christ loved the church. Any man who professes to be a Christian would first of all see you as his sister in Christ and secondly have enough of the fear of God for himself personally to be obedient in this area. Secondly, he should have enough respect for himself as a man of God to not to want to compromise the call of God on his life by engaging in relations without marriage. I knew all of this, but again because I had a faulty foundation and was incomplete in Christ, I allowed my heart to engage and fall in love with him anyway.

Without having the proper expectations in place at the beginning of a dating relationship, things can happen and then you find yourself repenting later. It is wise to be upfront about your choice to honor God by remaining abstinent at the very beginning. Any man that would want to date you should know this up front. If it is a problem for him, he will soon disappear. A man who really cares about you and is a true godly man will respect, appreciate and value this.

Jesus died a dishonorable death so that we could walk in honor as His daughters. He died for our dignity and honor. When we cross the boundaries that He died to protect, we are bringing shame to our Creator. He paid a very high cost with His life and the fact that we belong to Him makes us extremely valuable. As we grow and mature in Him and as we walk in our purpose as women of God, our value should continue to increase. Our value comes from who we are in Him as complete, whole, redeemed women. Our value increases in proportion to the extent in which we allow Christ to be fully formed in us and the degree to which we let Him transform our character. We cannot devalue ourselves by relaxing our boundaries in the name of romantic love.

Inside the book, What Women Don't Know and Men Don't Tell You, McKinney Hammond & Brooks says:

"There is a difference between price and cost. Price is a predetermined value set on something being offered for sale. In

*contrast, cost is determined by the total expense required in emotions and time spent, as well as what it takes financially to obtain and maintain the object of your desire...There is a difference between the price of a marriage license and the cost of being married...A man should have to count the cost to be with you...How much does your love cost? You've got to have your mind made up concerning your own value...**Cost prohibits experimentation** (emphasis added) **...As a woman, you are not a taste test...No man should be able to sample you and then decide if he wants to pay the cost associated with claiming you as his own**...You are priceless...You were created, redeemed and are deeply loved and valued by God...If being involved with you requires a high cost, you will be able to sift the wrong people out of your life...Understand your worth and know your value. Men use women who don't know their value (emphasis added)... (pp. 43-45).*

Girlfriend, it is time out for providing free test samples for your love in the name of keeping a man! Your love is worth so much more. Can I get an amen?

Boundaries with Your Life, Time, Talents & Treasures

Although, I had re-established my boundaries in regards to sex before marriage, I made a critical error in judgment which caused me to sit in a limbo, dead-end relationship with this minister for an additional three years. I failed to establish appropriate boundaries for my life. By doing this, I kept myself emotionally entangled with him when I should have ended it at the point when I saw that he did not care about my purity.

Because I still believed that we were going to get married "someday" and I continued to pray and work on being a good wife as I also over gave to him of my life, time, talent and resources. At the point in the relationship when it was clear that he had no intention of investing time to develop the relationship because he knew I was unwilling to compromise sexually, I should have also established the boundary that he would no longer have free access to my life as if he were my husband.

Instead, I gave him full use of my talents and skills that proved to be very beneficial to him as he began to rebuild his chaotic life. Because I wanted to be married, to love, and be loved so desperately, I set my value low unintentionally. I discounted and put my love on sale at a reduced rate. I allowed myself to be used in order to prove that I was worthy to be a wife. Not having strong boundaries in place made me open to his emotional manipulation. I went along with his agenda and ideas. According to him, all of the business related work I did was for "us" and "our" future, but I knew in my spirit and the back of my mind that somehow things were not adding up and that everything ultimately seemed to benefit him more than it benefited me. I had little to show for all of the effort, time, sweat, and tears I had poured into this relationship.

By not having strong boundaries, we can easily lose ourselves and get caught up in someone else's world because our identities have become blurred. We lose the edge that makes us unique and distinctive individuals. You can't be you if you are too busy shifting the boundaries that define you in order to keep someone else happy. This is what happened to me; however, because God was still working on me to help me see the truth, I was able to see what was happening.

I had to learn the hard way that I am to work for myself first. This means I am to allow God to work in and through me to bring me into complete healing and restoration before I am to be connected to serve another individual whom I desire to be my husband. Because my motives were impure (to get married), the giving of my talents and time did not benefit me at all but hurt me in the long run. I now realize that am to utilize my God-given gifts and talents to benefit myself and others in a healthy and balanced way. It also means I will not allow myself to be used by someone in the name of fixing, helping, healing, proving, validating or following a fantasy with nothing left to benefit me.

I learned the hard way that I am to be discreet, cautious and wise is it relates to the giving of my time, talents and treasure to a man without true commitment. Because I had soft boundaries and thought we would ultimately become married, I gave him the full benefit of my gifts, talents and resources while he had very little to pour back into me. This left me operating in a continual deficit while he was getting full.

Throughout the Gospels, Jesus provides plenty of examples of setting personal boundaries. Though He was God in the flesh, He realized that He was in a human body that required rest, food and sleep. He was aware that He lived in a natural earth with only 24 hours in a day and that He could only be in one city at a time. Jesus said "no" plenty of times to people who demanded more. When He moved on from one city to the next, some people did not get healed when He left. He didn't run around attempting to heal every single soul in each town. Not everyone got Jesus when they wanted Him. He slipped away quite often to pray alone. There are instances where He even required the people who asked for healing to go and do something. He didn't do all the work. They had to exercise faith. In other words, Jesus did what He needed to do to protect His anointing, guard His strength and keep Him going until He had to go to the Cross. What makes us think that we can be superwoman and be all things to all people (including our men) and split ourselves a thousand ways for validation, approval and romantic love?

Having clarity on your purpose as it relates to what you believe in your heart God desires for your life will help define your personal boundaries. Once you know where you are headed or at least ready to seriously pursue God to hear His heart in this matter, you will be in a position to define what you will or will not allow into your life. Becoming aware of, developing and using your unique gifts and talents will lead you towards your purpose in life. Once you become very purpose-minded, you will have little time for boundary busting behavior on your part or anyone else's. It will become extremely clear to you the people who will work in your life within the realm of your boundaries and purpose and those who do not. Take the time to get purposeful about your life and your boundary lines will become very clear.

The inverse of this is also true. If you are meandering about, waiting on a man, putting your life on hold for marriage, you will be prone to have soft boundaries in your desperation and neediness to be married. You will be more likely to have shifting boundaries, accept shady behavior and in general bend over backwards to please your mate because your goal is marriage, not pursuing your God-given purpose. Get clear on your purpose first and then the marriage according to God's timing and way will follow. *"Seek ye first the kingdom of God and His righteousness and all these things will be added unto you."* Matthew 6:33 (KJV)

Boundaries also play an important role in determining who gets close to you. Only those who qualify through trust established over time should be allowed in your inner circle. Do you have an inner circle or are you an isolated woman, doing your own thing because you don't trust other women as friends? People who show themselves godly, trustworthy and wise are the only ones who should be able to speak into your life. They are the ones who can call you out and hold you accountable when they see that you are engaging in boundary shifting behaviors.

Reflect on God's Word:

1. Matthew 5:37 (AMP). *"Let your Yes be simply Yes, and your No be simply No; anything more than that comes from the evil one."*

2. Luke 16:13 (NIV). *"No servant can serve two masters. Either he will hate the one and love the other, or he will be devoted to the one and despise the other."*

3. I Kings 18:21 (KJV) *"How long halt ye between two opinions? If the LORD be God, follow Him; but if Baal, then follow him." And the people answered him not a word."*

Things to Think About

1. When you say "Yes", mean Yes and when you Say "No", mean No without any apologies or compromise. This is called being honest. Boundaries become softened when we say "Yes", but deep down inside, we know that we should've said "No". Now we have compromised our integrity and busted our boundary. What situations have you said "Yes", when you wanted to say "No", and what did it cost you in the end?

2. You must prioritize your life in order to have boundaries. Who are you going to serve – Your Savior or the world? You can't do both. It's either God's Way or Your Way. Make a choice and prioritize accordingly. Once your purpose is clear and established, you will not have any confusion or duality as to what you should be doing with your life and what your priorities are. Having clear sense of purpose provides priorities. Priorities provide boundaries. Do you have a clear idea of your purpose? When you know your purpose you will create priorities to support and supplement that purpose. What are your priorities in life right now? Do your relationships and boundaries reflect that? If not, Why?

3. Take Time For Yourself to Get Clear On You. There are countless scriptures where Jesus withdrew from the crowds for solitude. (Read Mark 1:35 and Luke 4:42). Alone time is critical to in order to know who you are, and get it down deep on the inside. Often we buck against the alone times but it is

where we need to be in order for God to heal us. We need alone time to get the faulty foundation strong. We need the alone time to establish and maintain our boundaries. We need the alone time to know our purpose. If Jesus took the alone time, then it stands to reason that as His followers we need alone time too. Are you running from God? Do you always have to be running around doing stuff, watching TV, getting on Facebook, tweeting, texting, and surfing? If you are alone and the house gets too quiet, do you get uneasy on the inside? If you are alone or quiet for too long, do you find that feelings of sadness and hurt sometimes surface? That is your clue that you have some work to do.

Chapter 4
Lack of Wisdom In Dealing With Men

Godly wisdom functions as a preservative of life. The entire purpose of wisdom is to preserve, edify and increase life. Without wisdom or acting in the opposite of wisdom we reap corruption, decay and ultimately death in some form or fashion be it spiritually, mentally, emotionally, relationally, physically or financially. Lack of wisdom in the area of romantic relationships can be emotionally and spiritually devastating.

Wise Women Pay Attention to the Red Flags

Why is it so incredibly easy for us to ignore and gloss over very clear, strong and obvious red flags? The statement by Maya Angelou states it beautifully – *"When people show you who they are, believe them."* People can only maintain a façade for so long. Eventually their true colors will come out. Their behavior and their words will eventually be in conflict one another. There is no in between, gray area of justification or rationalization as to why their words and actions do not match. If a man tells you he loves you, but fails to show up for you 99% of the time, then suffice it to say that he does not love you. When a man shows up for you, it means that he is fully invested and committed to you and the relationship. He actually spends quality time with you. There is true friendship and companionship. He supports you in the good and the bad times of life. It is not just sex, romance and exchanges of money or resources. Being there and showing up means doing life *together*.

I have so many examples in the relationship with the minister where I allowed him to cancel plans at the last minute or he would call and say he was on the way but never showed up. For example, we never spent one single Christmas together as a couple. He would say he was going to come and make big promises that would never pan out. Ultimately, because we lived in different cities, we would meet halfway and have parking lot Christmas gift exchanges. Yet he claimed his undying love for me and that he intended to marry me. This went on for several years.

I remember one incident in particular that stands out in my mind because it happened right before my father passed away. For my birthday, my family had planned a surprise visit to my home. I was expecting only my parents to come, but I didn't expect to see my sister and her family. Also, on that same day, he was on his way to visit. This time he really was on the road to see me.

When he saw my parents' vehicle sitting in the driveway, he took an immediate U-turn and left. He did not want to face my family. Bear in mind that they have not seen him in a couple of years since he asked my dad for my hand in marriage. He always managed to make excuses and not show up for anything with my family. He called me right after he had made the U-turn while they were still at my house and basically said he didn't want to face them and there was no way he was going in the house or hanging out with us to celebrate my birthday.

Little did both of us know that it would be the last time I would see my father alive as well as the final gathering with my family before my father suddenly passed away three weeks later. Fortunately, I was able to move on that day, enjoy my family and spend quality time with them, but it hurt me deeply that he would be so selfish as to leave as soon as he saw my parents' car in my driveway. This was another red flag but again, I *chose* to ignore it.

When you really and truly love someone, you will want to be with them and your actions will line up. He said he loved me, but his actions displayed the opposite. He gave so many red flags in the beginning of the relationship, but I kept giving him the benefit of the doubt. As a result, it cost me much more than I could ever imagine. Had I paid attention I would have saved myself from a lot of heartache and pain.

Yes, we can give people the "benefit of the doubt," but we must become more sensitive and quickly take heed to the warning signs that we receive by the spirit and learn to trust it. When we keep overriding the nudges and prompts from what many of us like to identify as a "Woman's Intuition" (I call it the Holy Spirit), eventually we will not receive any warnings at all and will find ourselves in situations looking around wondering, "How in the world did I get here?" We will override and ignore to the point that we become deceived and then we stop trusting ourselves. This is a very dangerous place to live.

We do not need to have a logical explanation as to why something doesn't "set" right with us on the inside. It does not have to make sense to your brain. It doesn't matter if everyone else you know is doing it, going along with it, or seems to be okay with it. If you do not feel right, then trust that feeling. Do not try to figure it out or second guess. Trust it! You will be very glad that you did. Later on, you will see why and will soon discover that by obeying that prompting, you may have very well saved your life, a bunch of grief and anxiety, or from wasting time in another dead-end relationship. I have learned that if I am praying in the Spirit, staying in the Word of God, and trusting Him to lead me, He is indeed doing that and I can trust that warning or check in my spirit. I only have close relationships with people whose walk equals their talk and whose words and actions match. If I see otherwise, I exit quickly. In other words girlfriend, if it slides like a snake, if it slithers like a snake, then guess what? It is a snake! How many countless times did I spend praying trying to get an understanding on behavior that was flat-out wrong in an effort to make it make sense in my mind?

Because of overriding the checks in our spirit, we keep ignoring, making justifications and rationalizations of the shady behavior of some of our Christian men. We are the enablers of this if we continue to allow them to do it and make excuses for them in the name of Jesus. Jesus called a viper a viper. He was meek. He was nice and sweet to the woman who was about to be stoned. He was kind and compassionate to the woman with the issue of blood. He cast demons out of the man roaming in the cemetery. But he called the Pharisees a brood of vipers and ran the money changers out of the temple with a whip. He did not mince words or sugar coat things. So if He lives in us, how come we don't do what He did?

Wise Women Walk in Personal Integrity

Back in Chapter 1, we talked about having integrity as it relates to building a strong foundation in Christ. Let's take a more in-depth look at the word integrity. Integrity is taken from the root word "integer." An integer is a whole number. It is not a fraction or a decimal. If I am broken on the inside, I have internal fractions in my soul. Therefore, I lack true integrity or wholeness. Integrity is also defined as *"uprightness of character; uncompromising adherence to moral and ethical principles; a sound or unimpaired condition; the state of being whole or entire."* The word integrity also means "to prove" from the Latin meaning of the word probare which literally means *"to test to make something honest".*

The combination of the various meanings and subtle nuances of the word "integrity" opens our eyes to quite a few things. The meaning of this word as it relates to our lives as Christian women indicates that (1) we need Christ to make us whole and sound; (2) we must be tested in order for the integrity, wholeness and soundness to be proven.

Our choices in love relationships directly reflect the level of integrity that we are walking in. If our love relationships are ungodly, shady, suspect, secret, or compromising, then it indicates a lack of inner integrity. Remaining in such relationships is not always the fault of the men; it is our choice to continue in such a relationship, despite the fact that it is actually creating further brokenness. Michelle McKinney Hammond goes on further to state that *"Choice is a powerful dynamic in your life. When choosing, you are the master of your choice. After choosing, you are the servant of it."*

Time after time, we make the choice to remain in situations that do not reflect inner integrity. On top of that, we choose not to receive the integrity that Jesus died for us to walk in. Then when we must start serving that relationship choice and all the various consequences and side effects, we wonder why it is so painful.

The reality is that when we make deliberate choices to entangle ourselves in relationships that do not enhance our wholeness but bring further brokenness, we are living a lie. Integrity is walking in and living in the truth - your truth. You cannot have inner integrity but continue to lie to yourself about how great your man is when you know he is not and that you are hurting because of his ongoing hurtful behavior towards you. It's time to be real in order to be healed.

This is what I did in an attempt to reconcile in my mind the lack of congruency between his actions and his words. I tried to rationalize and justify how great he was based on the few good things he did right. However, this did not alleviate the pain. I was in denial and was lying to myself. How can you even begin to have integrity if you lie to yourself, live in denial, and refuse to look at the cold hard truth about your situation? Everyone else sees it – your family, your friends; people at work and church. The façade can only last but for so long.

Without filtering our minds – our very lives through the Word of God, we can very easily and unwittingly live out a lie. A life of truth and authenticity can only be lived through constant immersion in the Word of God. A human mind and heart, if left to its own devices, will always revert to self-deception. According to Jeremiah 17: 9-10 (NAS), *"the heart is more deceitful than all else and is desperately sick, who can understand it... I, the Lord, search the heart and I test the mind, even to give to each man according to his ways, according to the results of his deeds."* This is the very reason why Jesus came to save us. That is why we need Him. He came to not only to sacrifice his life for our sins, but to also provide the Holy Spirit, known as the Spirit of Truth to live and to dwell within us.

To deceive is defined as to cause to believe what is not true; mislead or to lead another into error, danger, or a disadvantageous position by underhanded means. If you are self-deceived then you are doing this to yourself. An example of this would be convincing yourself that your boyfriend is deeply in love with and is faithful to you while at time same time you are snooping around checking his cell phone and his pants pockets for evidence of cheating. A woman of integrity and wholeness would have quickly exited this relationship once she saw the red flags and found any evidence of cheating. A woman of integrity would have no need to be snooping around in the first place because she would have discerned his true nature from the beginning. A whole woman would accept the facts at face value and run for the hills! A broken woman would be hurt and angry but would eventually allow him to come back and convince herself that he is changed. She somehow thinks this man is telling her the truth. She genuinely expects a man to tell her the truth when she is living a lie herself.

When we are in self-deception, we are leading ourselves into error, danger and other disadvantages through an underhanded method in our own minds. It is like stabbing your own self in the back and then wondering who did it. By seeking the Lord and staying in His Word, we will grow into integrity and greater degrees of wholeness. To the extent that we walk in integrity, we will be able to more quickly identify brokenness and lack of integrity in others. "Like" attracts "like". If you are attracting a lot of broken men with serious issues, then the source lies from within – your own brokenness.

Also, as we immerse ourselves in the Word of God, prayer and fellowship with other believers, we will grow in wisdom, sound judgment and discretion. These are key character traits that work hand in hand with integrity that will help keep you from lying to yourself, making foolish choices and leaning to your own understanding instead of God.

Wise Women Exercise Sound Judgment

Sound judgment is defined as the capacity to assess situations or circumstances shrewdly and to draw sound conclusions. The word "shrewd" is defined as having keen or sharp awareness and/or to be clear-sighted. The meaning of "sound" in this context means conclusions that are based on valid reasoning; free from logical flaws; marked by showing common sense; levelheaded. Putting all of this together means that if we walk in sound judgment we will have the capacity to accurately assess our current relationship with clear-sighted awareness.

In Hebrews 4:12 (ESV), we read, "For the Word of God is quick and powerful and sharper than any two edged sword ...and is a discerner of the thoughts and intentions of the heart." With the Spirit of Truth in full operation in our lives through active study in the Word of God, we will have sharp minds and be able to discern the truth about our situations. With clear-sighted awareness, we will be able to draw logical, common sense and level-headed conclusions about whether or not the current relationship is complimentary and conducive for God's will in our lives and whether or not it will be ultimately harmful to us in the long-run.

The problem we have as women of God is that we allow our emotions, fantasies, feelings, baggage of the past and unmet emotional needs for completion to hinder our capacity to use sound judgment. How can we use sound judgment when our minds are beclouded with fantasies, visions of the future, wild emotions and feelings, lust, and baggage from previous relationships?

It is difficult because the feelings, imaginings, and desires of the heart are very strong. It takes the supernatural power of the Holy Spirit, immersion in the Word of God, and prayer to develop a clean heart that loves God first and foremost. It takes fellowship with other believers to help keep us accountable to the ways and wisdom of the Lord. Without this in operation, we are prone to allowing our fantasies, daydreams, desires and longings to become idols in our hearts. An idol is anything or anyone that you love, long for and desire more than Jesus Christ.

If we want to be married more than we desire God and the things of God, then marriage becomes an idol. Having the desire for companionship and a healthy marriage is not wrong, but when the desire becomes so strong that it supersedes your desire for God then it becomes a serious problem. As Carla R. Cannon states in The Power in Waiting, *"...Before the Lord can send you a mate, you must first learn to be content with Him first. The Word of God instructs us to love the Lord God with all of our heart, soul and mind...Our desire for a mate should not have more of our focus than the Lord has."* When the desire for a mate becomes more of our focus than God, it is at this point that sound judgment, wisdom and discernment will be taken over by folly, poor judgment and bad decisions. The choices made while these desires are on the throne of your heart instead of God will inevitably be disastrous.

Wise Women See Pass the Glamour & the Bling

Many Christian men, ministers, preachers, pastors, church leaders are broken and unhealed. They attract broken, lonely, and unhealed women who are in love with the lifestyle or image of being married to a godly man. As for myself, I was married to an unsaved man for ten years. I went to church Sunday after Sunday either alone or with my kids. For years I would sit in church and observe the other couples who came to church together holding hands. I felt sad and lonely in my faith walk because I really couldn't come home and share the sermon or talk about a scripture with my husband for his interpretation because to him it was all nonsense and foolery.

After the divorce, I began to pray and ask God for a godly man with whom I could go to church with and we could serve God together. When a man who not only professed to be a Christian, but also a minister expressed interest in me, I thought that it was an answer to my prayer. I became enchanted by the whole idea of possibly being a pastor's wife. Ladies, let's be real here. Am I the only one who liked the idea of being well-dressed and waltzing into church while everyone looks on with my godly man beside me?

Again, I was still broken and looking for marriage to feel complete. He was a very broken man and unable to give true love although he had a position in the church. Because of his position, my own brokenness and the simple fact that it was the first time I had a godly man as a potential husband, I failed to use wisdom or sound judgment.

If we are not walking as complete women in Christ and if we lack wisdom, we will lower our standards and shift our boundaries even when we can clearly see with our own eyes suspect behavior from our "man of God". We don't want to believe that what we are seeing is really true. We start to rationalize, make excuses and justifications for his behavior because we think he is special and the rules somehow don't apply to him, us, or our "special" situation and that standard reason – "God knows our hearts." We extend extra grace and pray more fervently for him in the hopes of change. We keep giving extra chances because it just doesn't make sense in our minds and we know it is not adding up but we want to hang on anyhow. This is what I did. I made excuses for his ongoing problems, chaos and overall inability or unwillingness to have a real relationship with me. I justified his behavior because he was under stress, financial strain, depression, and unresolved grief.

I automatically assumed that because he had a title, an appearance of financial resources, natural and spiritual gifts that it meant he could be trusted and that he knew what he was doing. It is nice to be associated with people who appear to have it all together, i.e., like they got it "going on" so to speak. The reality of this assumption is that no matter how much money, titles, positions, spiritual gifts and power a man has, he is still a human being complete with flaws. Only time can tell whether or not a man's position is built on a sure and stable foundation. Only time can tell whether or not he is totally secure in his identity as a child of God or whether or not his identity is based in his position, power or spiritual gifts.

Not only did I make the assumption that he had it altogether because of his position, but I also lacked the wisdom to know the difference between a person's spiritual fruit and their spiritual gifts. Gifts such as the ability to sing, preach, teach, exhort, play musical instruments and so on are given by God without repentance. The Fruit of the Spirit, however are grown in the soil of life under a variety of circumstances which are usually not pleasant. Spiritual fruit consists of love, joy, peace, patience, meekness and self-control. These are character traits that reflect the true nature of a person. Spiritual fruit is evidence of a person's character becoming more and more like Christ. As a whole and complete woman of God, you cannot afford to engage your heart with a man based on his gifts, but based on the fruit you see in his life. It is the fruit that you are going to be dealing with in the marriage, long after the allure of his gifts wear off.

I was guilty of this. I was beside myself when this man of God expressed his intent to marry me. I was caught up in the title and the fact that he appeared to have it all together on the outside. He was well-spoken, had a strong presence, really knew the Scripture and could preach. I overlooked the fact that he was still very broken and struggling. I thought he needed me and that I could help him heal and that we would ride off into the sunset as a happy couple serving God together. Somehow I managed to overlook the small fact that that he had a lot of unresolved issues, was grief-stricken, had a questionable background in previous relationships, and was clearly not ready to be married.

He revealed his true character very early in the game, but I was too full of my emotions and fantasies to really pay attention. I kept overriding that foreboding sense of anxiety. I allowed myself to be rushed along in romance and high feelings, but all the while in the back of my mind, I knew this situation was not the best. I was prideful and thought that I could "handle" it and that God would work everything out in the end because we loved each other and I sincerely desired to honor God. Let me tell you right now, no matter how you slice it or add it up - God can't bless mess!

Little did I realize that God is not obligated to honor mess that began with a lack of integrity. Little did I know that I was overriding the *"checks"* in my spirit. I learned the hard way that God will let you go full-steam ahead in your decision and He will let you feel and experience all of the consequences when you make a decision to override His prompts when all He was trying to do was protect you. Mandy Hale in the book, *The Single Woman* states:

...we find someone we like and who likes us, and although we might have a tiny sense of unease that something isn't quite right, we forge ahead, thinking we're just imagining things and overreacting. Before we know it, our tiny sense of unease turns

into foreboding, our foreboding into sheer dread, and then we find ourselves careening full steam ahead toward the crash of all crashes, simply because we didn't heed that still, small voice the first time it spoke up. When we run through a stop sign, what happens? Danger. Calamity. Chaos. Injury, to our person or to our emotions. So why do we stubbornly barrel toward a relationships that's not meant for us when your intuition is telling us otherwise?" (p.75)

When a woman prematurely engages her heart based on the outward appearance, she places herself in a very vulnerable position of not knowing who the real man is without the title, position, power or money. True character is revealed slowly in patterns over time. Before engaging your heart, take your time to observe his character in diverse conditions. If you were in a coma and could not make decisions for yourself would you trust this man to make decisions for your life, finances and children as a husband would? Is he moody and unstable? Do you really know who he is, or better yet does he know who he is without all the exterior trappings? Has he taken the time to heal from his past relationships? Is he on the rebound? Is he running from the call of God on his life? Are there a lot of gaps and question marks in his story? These questions must be answered before you get very serious. The quality of his character must be established as a critical component of a relationship leading to marriage. Jesus paid too high of a price to redeem our lives for us to make life-altering decisions without counting the cost and wisdom. Beloved, take your time to observe the fruit of his life before engaging your heart. Let not the outward façade fool you.

Wise Women Use the Weapon of Patience

In Ephesians 5:15-17 (KJV) we are admonished to *"walk circumspectly, not as fools, but as wise"*. The word *circumspect* means to be *"heedful of circumstances and potential consequences; prudent; watchful and discreet; cautious"*. The word circumspect is derived from the root Latin word "spec ere" which means to look around. The word tells us that we are to literally look around and be watchful in our relationships. In spite of this, we can often see that something is not quite right but we instead choose to put our blinders on in the name of love.

We are so ready to love and engage our hearts at the drop of a hat. We do not want to wait on God. We do not want to wait to see if this man is right for us. We do not have the patience to hold our emotions and feelings in check until we can really look and see what the real deal is. Prolific Bible teacher, Mike Murdock has stated, *"Patience is a weapon that forces deception to reveal itself."* Without the patience to wait on God and to see this man's true colors, we prematurely leap into an unknown situation and then realize when it's too late and the damage has been done to our hearts. We could've avoided the situation all together if we had just waited a little while longer before committing ourselves.

In the Power in Waiting, Carla Cannon lets us know that *"just any man can't have a woman of your caliber. We are beautifully and wonderfully made, created with destiny in mind, and God will not allow all of His hard work to be tainted by some Bozo. We must stop allowing people to lead us to believe that we are missing something because we choose to be selective in who we date and not jump on the first thing that comes our way..."* Being selective requires patience and wisdom. God always reveals and acts on our behalf if we simply exercised self-control and waited on him as shown in Isaiah 64:4(AMP) - *"For from of old no one has heard nor perceived by the ear, nor has the eye seen a God besides You, Who works and shows Himself active on behalf of him who [earnestly] waits for Him."*

A key patience test as to whether or a not a man is a high caliber, high character man is whether the speed in which he takes the relationship. A true, godly man will not, under any circumstances, attempt to prematurely rush the relationship. He walks in wisdom and will want to take his time in getting to know you. He will not try to rush into sex. He will not say a lot of things within the first few weeks that should only be said once you have known someone for a while. Even if in the early stages of a relationship, a man feels led by God to believe that you might be *"The One"*, he will still wait until he has received confirmation in his spirit. He may or may not reveal that to you at first. Also, there are testimonies of Christian couples who both knew that they had found *"The One"* early in the relationship, but even in those cases, they waited until they had both received confirmation. They did not jump out prematurely based on a feeling.

A man who is seriously considering you as a potential wife would take some time to observe how you act, your character and he will give you time to also observe and get to know him. He doesn't want to marry a crazy woman! You want a wise man who thinks long-term and who takes his time. There is no right or wrong time frame as to how long a man should wait before taking the relationship to the next level. It depends on both of the individuals involved, the complexity of their unique situation or circumstances and the readiness of both individuals for the demands of marriage.

From my perspective, I believe you can tell where a relationship will go within the first three to six months. You can tell whether or not there is enough friendship, substance, chemistry and sustainability for the long haul within that time frame. Also within that time frame is usually when most of the significant red flags will appear that will either put the brakes on the relationship or at least slow it down considerably. Looking back over my experience, I now realize that he gave the majority of his most serious red flags within the first three months.

As a godly woman, you want a man who can think pass the immediacy of the moment, hormones, and emotions because this will be very critical once you say *"I do."* A man who has ulterior motives will want to rush you along so fast that you can't think straight. He will try to fast forward the relationship in an effort to get what he wants which could be: (1) Sex, (2) an ego boost or stroke and lastly, (3) money and other resources from you. A man who is rushing the relationship along in a big whirlwind of romance, sweet talking, and sweeping you off your feet may also push your boundaries much more and create extra pressure on you. This is also a red flag. A true godly man who intends to love you like Christ loves the church will not under any circumstances want you to support him financially. It is unbiblical for a woman to support a man financially while he does nothing. The man is called to provide and protect. If a man is unwilling to take care of himself financially, than he is not husband material no matter how fine he is.

Reflect on God's Word

1. Luke 10:27 (KJV) *"And he answering said, Thou shalt love the Lord thy God with all thy heart, and with all thy soul, and with all thy strength, and with all thy mind; and thy neighbour as thyself."*

2. Matthew 7: 15 – 20 (NKJV) *"Beware of false prophets, who come to you in sheep's clothing, but inwardly they are ravenous wolves. You will know them by their fruits. Do men gather grapes from thorn bushes or figs from thistles? Even so, every good tree bears good fruit, but a bad tree bears bad fruit. A good tree cannot bear bad fruit, nor can a bad tree bear good fruit. Every tree that does not bear good fruit is cut down and thrown into the fire. Therefore by their fruits you will know them."*

3. Phil 4:8 (NIV) *"Finally, brothers and sisters, whatever is true, whatever is noble, whatever is right, whatever is pure, whatever is lovely, whatever is admirable—if anything is excellent or praiseworthy—think about such things."*

Things to Think About

1. Stay tuned to the Holy Spirit to keep your own heart clean and idol free. Make sure you love God first with all of your heart and not romance or being married first.

2. You will know a man by his fruit. Fruit takes time to be seen. You will know who is in control of a man's life (the Holy Spirit or his sinful, carnal nature) by the fruit you see manifesting in his life. This takes time to observe and cannot be seen in a few days or weeks. It cannot be seen based on the words coming out of his mouth no matter how sweet they may sound. It cannot be seen based on how much scripture he quotes, how often he attends church, how he can pray, preach, teach, sing, play an instrument and testify. It can be seen in his ACTIONS. It can be seen through the life he lives before others; not only you. It can be seen in how others think, react and respond to him and his reputation.

3. Utilize wisdom and sound judgment as discussed previously. Don't be stupid, naïve or gullible. It is important that you keep your mind occupied and busy with living out the purpose of God for your life so that you do not have the man occupying too much mental and emotional space in your head and heart. Train your mind to think on the things of God. Utilize the wisdom and sound mind God gave you.

Part Two: Get Healed -- A Whole Woman Will Attract A Whole Man

Chapter 5
You Are Not Florence Nightingale

You attract what you are. To attract a healthy, whole man, you must be healthy yourself. If you have been attracting men with serious character defects and unresolved issues, you must first look within. The questions to ask yourself are: (1) What kind of signal am I giving off subconsciously or that I am unaware of that somehow draws the wrong kind of men? Why is it that I am always attracted to a certain type that I know deep down on the inside is not God's best for me? Is there a pattern to all of my relationships? If so, what do I need to do to break this pattern for once and for all? It is easy to verbalize that you are waiting on your Boaz and that you are ready to get married, but yet we keep fooling around with the wrong ones, wasting our time and getting our hearts bruised and damaged in the process. For me, the re-occurring pattern in this relationship was the overriding desire to bring healing and to help my man. I wanted to be his healer so that we could get married.

I was also very attracted to men who were the exact opposite of what I had dealt with in my previous marriage. I wanted a Christian man who would go with me to church. I hated going to church by myself all the time. I also enjoyed helping and showing how much I loved and cared through my actions. I romanticized the idea of helping my man rebuild his life so that we could be a testimony of what God could do as we rode off in the sunset together.

Florence Nightingale was an 18th century woman who was the pioneer of what is now the modern day nursing profession. She was known for going out at night with her lamp to nurse wounded soldiers back to health again. Nightingale dedicated her life to the entire field and study of statistics, sanitation, nursing and social reform. She conducted a great work of reform and risked her life in the midst of very squalid, dirty and unclean conditions in order to nurse wounded men back to health, especially during the Crimean War in 1854. Because she believed that she was called by God to do such a noble work, she never married. She was a true nurse in the highest form of the word in which her overriding desire was to bring healing to others even if it meant risking her own life and at her expense.

As women of God, we are called to have compassion, to help others, and to be a blessing for causes much greater than ourselves and some of us, like Florence Nightingale, may dedicate our lives without ever becoming married. Leading such a life of exemplary service and sacrifice is the highest calling of a believer. If you are reading this book, however, it would be safe to say that you are indeed very interested in becoming married one day and you likely do not wish to live as Florence Nightingale did.

In the arena of male and female relationships, it is not always very wise to function in a nursing/healing type of a role if your desire is to be found and pursued by a healthy and true Boaz. As a purposeful, godly woman it would not be wise to spend a lot of spiritual, emotional and mental energy to bring healing or to fix someone for the ultimate purpose of marrying them. Functioning the way that Florence Nightingale did within the realms of a romantic relationship by risking your own emotional and spiritual health is not God's highest and best will for his precious daughters.

As women, we were created with the innate capacity to nurture, comfort, build up and support others. For those of us who are spirit-filled, we cannot help but be touched with compassion when we see emotional and spiritual suffering and we know that we can do something about it. However, it can become very dangerous when we allow our compassion and desire to stand by a man cause us to do things to hurt ourselves. We were created to be a man's helpmeet, not his spiritual and emotional nurse. There are some things that only God can do. We must stop trying to play the role of God and remain in our lane in order to be effective in the areas in which we were created to operate in as women.

God did not call us to nurse a wounded man back to health (emotionally, spiritually, mentally, financially, business or otherwise) and then turn around and marry him. Yes, a godly sister can be very instrumental in helping a brother get back on track, however, there is a difference between allowing God to use you to minister to your brother in Christ in a healthy, balanced way while he is in need and ministering with mixed motives or underlying feelings. We must make sure that we are led by the Spirit and not our emotions and desires for a Boaz.

When God created woman, he took her from the Adam's side. He had to put Adam to sleep and create a wound in order to create Eve from his rib. The wound that was created had to be healed first. Adam remained asleep while his wound was being healed *before* he saw Eve to name her as his wife. Adam did not jump up from his sleep, still bleeding and wounded to go and find Eve. He remained at rest until he was healed by God and then found his wife. Eve did not go waking him up prematurely from his sleep or try to mess with the wound herself, but she waited on God to finish the work in her and to heal Adam before she actually became his wife. We jump out of spiritual order when we try to heal a man ourselves in our own efforts because we want to be married, instead of letting God finish his work in that man's life.

According to Ephesians 2:6 (KJV), you are seated in heavenly places with Christ. In addition, you are a daughter of the King. This means you are not to go beneath your position of being seated in heavenly places and risk getting yourself emotionally wounded in order to help a man who is not really serious about helping himself. The man God has for you would have already done his internal work and would be actively engaged in the process of rebuilding his life or pursuing his purpose. He would have enough wisdom to discern that he needed to get his own mess resolved before dragging an innocent, godly, compassionate woman in his business to help him.

This was my situation. I was in a Florence Nightingale pattern and it was reflected in my choice to stay in a dead-end relationship for too long. I had my wounded soldier and I was determined that with my help and love, he would become healthy and strong again. I sincerely desired to help him become the man of God he was called to be and I believed I could help him fix, heal and rebuild his life from scratch. However, I lacked wisdom and had plenty of my own issues to deal with. How do we look, carrying all of our own un-dealt with issues and baggage plus a man's baggage too? In my mind's eye, I can now see myself with all of my suitcases and bags, barely able to walk around with my own stuff and then I saw my Boaz and grabbed his suitcases and baggage too! Now I'm walking around hot, sweaty and struggling while he, on the other hand, is walking quite free and unencumbered. Child, I was a mess!

The need to "fix" or "heal" him revealed a certain pride and a need to fix someone in order to for me to feel good on the inside. It is vital to learn to feel good about yourself because of who you are in Christ, not because of your ability to fix or help a man. Your need to heal him is a result of you needing to fix, help and heal yourself. This is the true essence of the Florence Nightingale pattern --- bringing healing to someone else when you are wounded or unhealthy yourself. In their book, *What Women Don't Know and Men Don't Tell You*, Michelle McKinney Hammond & Joel A. Brooks Jr. share:

"You cannot have a complete relationship with an incomplete man, and you usually can't recognize his brokenness until you are fixed. Until you are whole, you will find yourself actually attracted to his neediness. You will feel compelled to take on his wholeness as your assignment and then internalize the shame when you fail;

because you will fail. The truth is that, when you take on his lack of wholeness, you are superimposing your own brokenness onto him. You are really trying to fix yourself. Instead, your healing must begin with allowing God to free you from your fantasy and change your life from the inside out...." (p.37)

He needs to acknowledge, seek after and receive his own healing. He can't do this if you are all in the way, enabling him, puffing up his ego to help his wavering self-esteem and cleaning up behind his mess, making excuses for him. If you try to heal him, which will always result in you relaxing your boundaries to "help" him, you will pay a stiff price because you will be enabling him at the expense of your own healing and growth. At the end of the day, you will be left emotionally bankrupt because you made more withdrawals, giving to fix him, but alas, he only had a few measly scraps to re-fill you. Plus, he knows deep down inside that he really doesn't respect you for doing this. Get rid of the idea that if he sees how great you have stood by him in the midst of his chaos and mess that somehow he will wake up and smell the coffee that you are The One. Men tend to lose respect when women do this.

Speaking directly from my own experience, I found myself in a situation where I was constantly lifting my significant other up in prayer for his issues and struggles, but my own needs and issues remained unresolved. The only thing I really wanted was for God to complete the healing process in him so that we could move forward and get married as I thought we would. I couldn't see that the fact that if he really cared about being healed of his own issues, that he would actually take the steps to seek God for himself, do better and be better instead of making excuses, talking a good game, and stringing me along.

In light of all of this, I now realize the long-term side effects and implications of not being rooted and grounded in the love of God for so long. I realize that the lack of a deep inward knowledge of how much Jesus really loved me is what created the insecure, anxious love and caused me to do things out of a perceived need. The reality was that I had everything I needed in Christ to start with but really didn't know it or tap into it. This has played out in my romantic choices. In my neediness to have a man, I asked God for a man of God who "needed" me. Then I thought I hit the jackpot with him. I was too naïve and too broken to have proper discernment. In my eyes, I finally had the opportunity to marry a godly man and we could serve God together. Being married was on the throne of my heart -- not God.

Living like this over a long period of time left me emotionally and spiritually depleted, because I could see no tangible results for my ultimate desire which was to be married, but instead the only results I saw was that he was getting better, but at my expense. I could feel bitterness and resentment creeping in because I began to feel very low emotionally with nothing left to give. The better he felt about himself, the worse I felt and he began to treat me with less respect.

Interestingly enough, the lights finally came on when I finally broke down and had the courage and grace to humble myself, and be willing to let go of my fantasy and hidden agenda with him. I totally and completely handed that relationship and all of the prayers, sweat, emotional and spiritual equity I had invested into this man over to God. Then God began to open my eyes and thus began the healing process which ultimately enabled me to let go and move on.

A healthy man that has resolved his issues should be able to provide you with the same level of lifestyle and standard that you currently provide for yourself as a single woman or higher. He will not be perfect but you should not have to experience a declination in your life in order to help raise him up emotionally, spiritually and financially. He should already be at a certain level when you arrive into his life. He should be able to provide for you spiritually, physically and emotionally as the leader. You should not have to piece him together and then expect him to feed you afterwards. He should be able to provide food, clothes and shelter. You should at the very minimum feel safe and secure with him. There are different situations that require discernment. If you truly pray and sense that he is sincere, is in a temporary setback and his intentions are honorable, that is different. There is a reasonable give and take that is to be expected if you are to be a true friend and potential partner. But you must still guard your heart and be discerning. If he cannot hold his own as a man at any consistent level then he cannot be considered for marriage, no matter how fine he is, the words coming out of his mouth, his excuses, or how much Bible he quotes, his job or how talented he is. If you see signs of raggedy and rinky-dink behavior in the areas of keeping a job, managing finances and spiritual/emotional growth & capacity, it is time to flee.

Reflect on God's Word

1. Matthew 7:6 (NLT) *"Don't waste what is holy on people who are unholy. Don't throw your pearls to pigs! They will trample the pearls, then turn and attack you."*

2. Ephesians 2:6 (NKJV) *"And hath raised us up together, and made us sit together in heavenly places in Christ Jesus."*

3. Proverbs 16:18 (NIV) *"Pride goes before destruction, a haughty spirit before a fall."*

Things to Think About

1. Review your past relationships that have failed. Is there a Florence Nightingale pattern in operation? Are you attracted to men who "need" you for something all the time (and we're not talking about sex)? Does this make you feel good and worthy? Are you are seated in heavenly places in Christ Jesus, full and complete in Him? Did you deliberately step down

yourself from your Queenly position to help a good man who is hurting and looks like Boaz potential? If he is your true Boaz, then he should be seated in heavenly places right up there with you, and if he is not, then you need to go back, get in your position, and leave that man where he is. He must desire to come up higher first.

2. Take a piece of paper and jot down on one side all of actual time, emotional energy, prayers, tears, running around, huffing and puffing, sweat, administrative work, cooking, cleaning, business stuff, job stuff, money given, loans, and whatever else you can think of that you have done for this man. On the other side write down all the things he has done for you that is tangible, meaningful and that actually COST him something in terms of time, energy or money. Compare the two lists. Is it out-of-balance and lopsided? If so you are a Florence Nightingale! The first step in breaking out of this is go to Christ and let Him heal you first. Take the time to get back in proper order as His daughter. Take the time to replenish your soul and become whole in Him first. Then you will have the grace and courage to break the pattern and get out of the dead end relationship.

3. At the end of the day, did these relationships leave you more depleted, confused and lonely than you were before you met them? Being in love should feel and actually be good. You should be better. Your whole life should be uplifted and better when the right man is present. Your entire lifestyle should UPLEVEL not DOWNSHIFT if he is the right one.

Chapter 6
How to Have Healthy Relationships

To attract positive relationships in general, you must be a positive person with a life of purpose. It takes deep soul-searching to really understand and know your purpose – what you believe in your heart that God has placed you on earth to do with your life. It is more than just using your gifts and talents (although that it is a significant part of it). It is all about who you are at your core --- the person you were meant to become. Once the "being" part of your purpose is established, then the "doing" part falls into place. You have to become the person God called you to be before you can do anything that will add value to His Kingdom and to the lives of others.

In saying all of this however, it will not be an overnight process. It takes time to go through the muck and mire of our past, to heal and forgive ourselves and others, to lean in and really unravel who we are on the inside. Many of us are afraid to go through this because it is scary and painful. Once you truly engage in the healing process, the pain passes quickly. However, it is far more painful in the long run to stay stuck than it is to go through the pain of healing and come out on the other side whole, healthy and strong.

The most important person to have a healthy relationship after God is with yourself. You must become your own best friend. You must treat yourself very nicely and be good to yourself. This means cutting out the negative self-talk that continually runs in your mind. We talk about ourselves internally worse than we would ever talk about someone else. This must stop if you are ever going to live in your purpose and glorify God with your life. The best way to honor the fact that Jesus died on the cross for you is to actually live your best life to the fullest without being stuck in a dead-end situation, beating yourself up with negative self-talk and not improving yourself for His glory. If we do not bring Him honor, we certainly are not honoring ourselves. We honor God by first honoring ourselves as His daughters.

Once you have done the work to become clear on who you are and your purpose, you are in a position to attract the right kinds of relationships. True relationships that are positive and healthy start off as solid friendships on mental, emotional and spiritual level. This too takes time to achieve. So often, we want to get all deep with a man very quickly because we like the immediate sense of emotional intimacy it provides. Sometimes it is much easier to open up to someone that does not know you very well and it can create a sense that you have known someone a long time. However, in reality, the relationship is still in its very early stages. No matter how much someone appears to be your soul mate based on the initial connection, time will always tell the true nature of the relationship. Remember that time is your best friend. As Author, Kim Brooks states in her book, *How to Date and Stay Saved*, *"Time always tells. Let Time tell it!"*

In addition to cultivating solid, healthy relationships with God and yourself, we must also cultivate healthy relationships with other women, guard our hearts with our Christian brothers, and learn how to get along with or get over the ex-boyfriend, ex-fiancé, ex-husband or baby's daddy,

But I Don't Want Anybody in My Business

As we grow and heal, it is very wise to continue to develop healthy relationships with other godly women and our families so that we do not isolate ourselves or allow the new relationship with a man to dominate our lives. It is important to have healthy relationships with other individuals that we trust outside of our dating relationship that know who we are and are familiar with our story so they can love and speak truth to us. We need a solid inner circle of people in our lives that really care about us regardless of whether we have a man or not. These kinds of relationships with other women and our families are so critical to our development and overall well-being. A bunch of people is not necessary, only a small, solid inner circle of people who will love us and speak the truth to us is what we need. Life is not meant to be lived in isolation. Award winning author, Sophia A. Nelson states in her book *Black Woman Redefined: Dispelling Myths and Discovering Fulfillment in the Age of Michelle Obama* states:

"...The key for us as black women of a new generation, however, is to understand that we must be truly interdependent as well as independent in how we support, love, counsel, admonish, encourage, and care for one another. Many of us will go it alone for most if not all of our lives, and as such we will need a caring community of women friends who will love us, rebuke us when needed, care for us, and be there for us..."

We often use the reason *"I don't want anyone to know my business or be in my business"* as an excuse because we have been hurt in the past when we told others details about our lives, especially if we are having problems in our relationship with our men. Because of this, we face hard times without support when all we had to do was reach out and ask for help. Oftentimes a word of wisdom, a key piece of knowledge or insight could be right in the mouth of someone we know, but because we want to "keep our business to ourselves", we often suffer in silence. Sometimes we endure bad relationships and make poor choices that keep us unhealthy because we isolate ourselves from the very ones who could help us.

Speaking from my own experience, my chief problem has been in isolating myself. By nature, I tend to be quiet and keep to myself, not out of meanness or being aloof, but sometimes pride --the kind of pride that says, I don't want people to know my business because I am ashamed of my stuff and a combination of just not being the type of person to go around opening myself up to everyone I meet. One of the main things that has actually helped me realize firsthand the importance of having someone who knows your business is the fact that when I found myself going through things in the weird dead-end relationship I was in, I looked around and realized that because I really wasn't truly open about my situation I lacked true community. I had put all my "emotional eggs," so to speak, in the holey basket of a man who lacked the emotional capacity to handle his own issues. I found myself left alone with the cracked eggs because I was too proud to solicit advice or ask for help. Now if I had the sense enough to keep and maintain open communication with trusted friends, I would have likely ended the relationship much earlier.

To really grow as a woman of God and attract a godly man, it is imperative to have godly female friends in your life to share wisdom, provide godly advice, pray with you and hold you accountable. This will help keep you when times get tough as you wait on the full manifestation of what you are believing God for as it relates to your relationship. Birds of a feather flock together. As you spend time with other godly women, you will increase in godliness, wisdom and virtue which will in turn attract the right kind of man. Not only must we cultivate healthy and godly relationships with other women, but we must also learn how to become friends with men without tripping and thinking that he is *"The One."*

I thought he was going to be" THE ONE" But He said We're Just FRIENDS

This can be tricky sometimes if you find that you really like someone. Is it possible to truly have a "brother in Christ" without having a secret crush on him or fantasizing about it turning into more? Many women claim that they have many such male friends that they are able to "hang out" with or talk to without it leading to anything. Others of us are not quite so sure. It is a fine balance of knowing your boundaries, guarding your heart, knowing how to carry yourself and really being able to discern his true intentions and expectations towards you. We participate and "help" our brothers in church events, singles groups and other ministry activities while thinking that we have our emotions and feelings under control, but are we really doing these things with pure motives? In the book, *Lady in Waiting* by Jackie Kendall and Debby Jones we read:

"...You must consciously resist doing another good deed for a man in your life until you know the motive behind your "unselfish" gesture. How many gifts have you already given to some guy in your life because you sense that the relationship had future dating potential? How many ministries have you participated in because of the chance to be seen by him? How many times have you volunteered to help a brother when you knew you would not be so willing to help a sister in Christ?"

It is extremely easy to get caught up in a situation with a Christian male friend – being there for him, helping him, listening to his problems, praying with him, doing good works together, all the while thinking you are being a good "Sister In Christ" to him; but your emotions and fantasies remain unchecked. Then, alas, he has great news to tell you-- his best friend, that he is engaged to be married to another woman! Now you are emotionally devastated and crushed. After all you have given of yourself to help build him up, be his friend and counselor, and all you are left with is a hug and a thank you.

According to Kendall and Jones, single Christian women defraud themselves of their own contentment in Christ by failing to heed what they call the "Eleventh Commandment." Simply put, the Eleventh Commandment is *"Thou Shalt Not Defraud Thyself."* They state that

"...Women defraud themselves by confusing ministry with matrimony. A guy tries to help a girl grow spiritually, and she sees his care and interest as leading inevitably to marriage. Another guy and girl work on a ministry team together and their spiritual intimacy is confused in her mind with romantic intentions...Misread intentions between males and females put them on a collision course. The crash can be avoided if the Lady of Contentment would keep in mind that her emotions must be submitted to the facts (emphasis added): ministering together is a privilege as a believer, not an automatic marriage opportunity...Daily, throughout the world, women's hearts are broken because they allow their emotions to run ahead of commitments..."

As a woman who has learned hard lessons from being in a limbo relationship, this very issue was a weakness for me. There is a reasonable amount of imagination that is inevitable when you meet someone you like, are attracted to, and there is mutual interest (or so it seems). However, it really takes having your heart submitted to Christ in order to resist the temptation to run for the hills in fantasy just because you have met a Christian brother that looks like a potential Boaz. Without being rooted in Christ and having solid boundaries, a single woman, no matter how strong she is, can easily get caught up and defraud herself through her own fantasies and unrealistic expectations. This is why having godly female friends is so important. Godly women will help you keep unrealistic fantasies in check as well so that your emotions don't run ahead without commitment.

In addition to having healthy friendships with other women and being wise in your relationships with Christian brothers, you must first be emotionally, physically, and spiritually free from the ex-boyfriend, ex-fiancé, ex-husband or baby's daddy if you desire to attract a godly man. It is a significant process to heal and move on from a previous relationship but it is imperative to do so if you wish to attract the man that God has for you. If you have children by your ex, it is important to be able to get along with him for the sake of the children. Also, when you meet the man that God has for you, it will be much easier if you and your ex have a positive relationship without drama that could potentially harm your new, healthy relationship.

Being Friends With Your Ex

You two don't have to be best buddies, but for the sake of the children, it would be extremely helpful if you could speak with him on a friendly basis without drama. It would make the lives of your children and your life easier in the long run – especially when you do meet and marry your Boaz in the future. How awkward would it be if you are still not getting along with your ex in that situation? For some of us we need to deal with the emotional wounds and get healed from the relationship so you can at least talk to him in peace regarding issues with the children. Again, the goal is not to be best friends, but to mutually co-parent the children in a respectful way. There will be bumps in the road. There will be disagreements. If he is unsaved, it may be more challenging. Nonetheless, it is worth it for the sake of your children to see that Mom and Dad are able to be civil and talk to each other without screaming and yelling all the time.

I do not claim to be an expert in this area. Speaking from my own experiences has not been easy. There have been times where we got along okay and then something would be said or done that would create conflict and it seemed like I was back at square one, not really speaking to him. Then it would get a little better and we would limp along. Overall as the years progressed we have gotten better, but it is still a work in progress. No good thing comes easy, but we are able to talk to each other as necessary. The trickiest part in this is that your ex may have unresolved issues towards you that he has not dealt with or is refusing to deal with or doesn't even realize that he has. This may be shown in his attitude towards you no matter how much you have prayed and worked on your own healing and forgiveness towards him.

If you did not have children with your ex, why would you want to be friends with him? There are several viewpoints on this subject that are too long to go into here. However, I believe that it depends upon how the break-up happened, the time spent apart after the break up, and whether or not you have fully healed from and gotten over him. It also is a function of whether or not you have cut the soul tie if you were sleeping with him. You cannot expect to be "just friends" with someone when you are still engaging in sexual activity with them. You cannot expect to be friends with someone in which you are still very angry and hurt towards. It just doesn't work that way.

If the break-up was handled in an amicable and mature way, it seems reasonable to expect that you could be respectful acquaintances or friends after a decent period of time of no contact. This is especially important if this ex is someone who works in the same building that you do or someone that you see frequently at work, church or in the community. You've got to be able to see him in public without acting weird and feeling funny.

However, if the break-up was messy and you still have feelings for him, he has not left you alone, you are still texting, talking, and going through changes, then (1) you are not fully done with the relationship and (2) you are holding up your own healing process. The key to friendships with ex-boyfriends is to establish a period of no-contact so that you can get healed, grieve and move on. The no-contact period is important because it allows you to have clarity on what went wrong in the relationship, your own issues that contributed to the break-up and it gives you some breathing space. This cannot occur if you let your emotions and hormones cause you to call him, text him, reply and respond to his communications. There is a reason why this relationship did not work. It doesn't mysteriously go away just because you miss him. The original problem that caused the break-up still exists. It did not disappear! Don't go back and keep digging it up, reviving it again based on the past crumbs, emotions, the ole' good times and feelings. Let it go. Once you have been able to fully let it go, then you may be able to talk to him without getting all caught up again. This time frame can vary from person to person, relationship to relationship. Let God guide you and keep your close godly friends around you to help you discern.

Reflect on God's Word

1.   Ecclesiastes 4:9-12 (NIV) *"Two are better than one, because they have a good return for their labor: If either of them falls down, one can help the other up. But pity anyone who falls and has no one to help them up. Also, if two lie down together, they will keep warm. But how can one keep warm alone? Though one may be overpowered, two can defend themselves..."*

2.   2 Corinthians 10: 5-6 (NLV) *"We break down every thought and proud thing that puts itself up against the wisdom of God. We take hold of every thought and make it obey Christ."*

3.   Romans 12:18 (KJV) *"If it be possible, as much lieth in you, live peaceably with all men."*

Things to Think About

1.   Are you functioning as a positive, wholesome person? Why would positive, vibrant, visionary men and women want you in their lives as a friend or as a potential mate if you are stuck in a rut emotionally, spiritually and with your life in general? What do you have to bring to the table other than unresolved issues, anxieties, and neediness that would drag them down and cause them to keep you at a distance? Remember birds of a feather flock together!

2.   Un-dealt with emotional wounds are toxic and cause us to remain emotionally and spiritually immature and unhealthy. We can look at emotional healing as a process in which a person is restored to integrity (wholeness) by first removing the dead stuff (sins -- hatred, bitterness, resentment, un-forgiveness, blaming others, unresolved grief, sadness, unruly passions and other deadly heart issues) with viable tissue – love, joy, peace, patience, and other fruits of the spirit. Ask the Holy Spirit to reveal the heart issues that are making you toxic and unattractive.

3.   Are you still emotionally or physically entangled with an ex-boyfriend, ex-fiancé or ex-husband in some type of way? This must be resolved and dealt with before you can attract a whole and healthy man of God into your life. Do you lack true friendships with other women because you are always "falling out" with someone and you don't trust anyone and of course,

you don't want anybody in your business? How has this hampered your life? Do you think this is God's best for you?

Chapter 7
Develop a Life of Poise - No More Confusion

When we are fully functioning at our highest and best level, our lives take on a certain sense of poise and order that manifests in how we conduct and carry ourselves. *Poise* is defined as a state of balance or equilibrium and composure under strain. It is also defined as a dignified, self-confident manner or bearing; composure and self-possession. *Order* is defined as a state in which all components and elements are arranged logically, comprehensibly, or naturally such that proper functioning or appearance is achieved. Chaos is defined as complete confusion and disorder; a state in which behavior and events are not controlled by anything, disarrangement and messiness.

As women of God, who are steadily progressing in our walk with Him, we should also be growing in the overall poise and order in our lives. Our lives should become more balanced (poise) and increase in overall proper functioning (order). As discussed in Chapter 5, we are daughters of the King and seated in heavenly places with Him. Our lives should reflect our dignity and our royalty. We can never be poised and pulled together if we are: (1) running from our issues and using people and earthly things to fill us emotionally and spiritually (2) getting up from our heavenly position to chase down an immature man and (3) staying in dead-end relationships that are not going anywhere but bringing us further down.

We lose a great deal of poise and self-confidence when we engage in these behaviors because it causes us to wear our feelings on our sleeves as we chase and prove to a man that we are "the one." We become emotionally unglued because we are always worrying, manipulating, strategizing, and trying to figure out what to do next in our relationship. We cannot live a poised and pulled together life because we are too busy running around trying to catch and keep a man all the time. We run from God when He tries to deal with us. We don't have time for quiet reflection, prayer and bible study which serve to increase our peace and poise as we daily seek God. The more a woman spends time with God, the more peaceful and poised on the inside she becomes. The less she spends time with God, the more anxious, emotional and open to self-deception she becomes.

When a woman is composed and self-possessed, it means that she is in control of her mind, body and her emotions. She does not allow the pressure of external circumstances and outside individuals to disturb or disrupt her internal order on the inside. This kind of woman has made a non-negotiable decision to live her life intentionally according to the design as revealed by God for her life. She is not walking haphazardly, by default, from crisis-to-crisis, relationship to relationship on a whim. She has decided what kind of woman she is going to be, how she wants her life to look, and what changes need to be made in order to achieve it. She actually goes for it and walks it out. She doesn't let her desire for marriage to cause her to deviate from the woman she knows she is to be on the inside. She is led by the Spirit of Truth – the Holy Spirit to help keep her in all these things. This is a woman of great poise and order.

The cultivation of greater degrees of composure and self-possession is not something that happens overnight. It occurs in degrees over time as woman deliberately makes the effort to grow, to change and to renew her mind. There is no way that any human being can grow in poise and it manifest in the outward areas of life, without first dealing with the mind. The mind must be continuously renewed over and over again. This is no easy feat and it is a lifetime endeavor. It requires deep soul-searching and dealing with painful issues in order to unearth the truth about ourselves, receive the healing, and move on. Again, this takes time and is not easy. The end result is greater freedom and confidence which is the backbone of having true poise. A poised and self-controlled woman is a very confident person on the inside. It is not a confidence that is of the cocky, arrogant sort, but a humble confidence, a balanced confidence that realizes where the Source of true strength and power comes from – God.

This confidence is not only borne out of resolving issues but also comes from really discovering your strengths, gifts and talents. In this process you grow in confidence as well. Eunice Leong-Tan in her book, *Secrets of Elegance* states:

"...The confidence grows as you pursue your interests with a new surge. You will be in your zone, your element... A certain authority develops, a secure, quiet self-assurance will be yours to possess...You are not just becoming more of yourself, but you are growing into your fullest potential. That is how God envisioned you when He first made you. To be true to yourself is to be authentic...We become comfortable in our own skin. We can stop being self-conscious and focus on others. This is one of the fundamental roots of an elegant (poised) woman..."

Again, the opposite person – unbalanced, weak, disorganized, confused woman--is also likely to be very insecure and have lots of un-dealt with issues floating around just beneath the surface of her life. This type of woman has not taken the time to really dig deep and to find out what her true strengths, gifts and talents are; but she may have an inkling or a clue. She may be dabbling in it a little, but allow fears and the opinions of others to keep her from fully leaning in and pursuing it. So her life may just stay in an overall limbo cycle of disorder, fear and confusion.

A lot of women appear to have it going on initially, but when the pressures of life hit, you will see the real deal of who they really are and the lack of poise and order will be very apparent. As women of God, we cannot afford to be like this and think that God will promote us to higher levels in life. In this disorganized mentality and lifestyle, we cannot be trusted to handle anything of significance with regards to His Kingdom agenda. We cannot be put on public display if our lives are in disarray. Not only that, as long as our lives are in disarray, we are out of position for God to send us the man He has for us. Ouch! It's time out for running around like chickens with our heads cut off and get ourselves together if we expect to walk in God's purpose and be ready for Boaz!

If we are in a state of confusion about our lives and our purpose, we will not have the capacity to receive the man that God has for us if he showed up. We would either repel him from the beginning or we would inadvertently self-sabotage the relationship because of our issues. Bear in mind that God loves your potential Boaz just as much as He loves you. He wants the best for His sons. A wife is designed to be a crown to her husband (Proverbs 12:4). She cannot be a crown if she is messy. God will not allow His beloved son, your potential Boaz to connect with you if you are functioning in this state.

The inverse is also true. We absolutely cannot afford to tolerate this in the lives of a man whom we are considering as a potential mate or we would be dishonoring ourselves and God. Once you have begun the process of increasing your overall poise as a woman by digging deep and designing your life according to God's purpose for you, you must be aware of the signs of confusion, where it comes from and how it operates in relationships so that you can avoid being entangled in such a relationship. When you realize your value and the high price that Jesus paid for you to live an abundant, purposeful, peaceful and poised life, you must exercise caution in who you allow into your life, and in particular men who have underlying confusion and chaos.

Men who always have some type of drama or chaos in their lives provide plenty of red flags, clues and traces that will let you know right away that you should avoid them. Because of their proclivity to make poor decisions or engage in confusing behaviors, it tends to breed a perpetual state of appearing to go backwards or in circles in their life and in the relationship as a whole instead of moving forward.

Being in a Dead-End Relationship Creates Inner Confusion

Limbo is defined as a region or condition of oblivion or neglect; a state or place of confinement; an imaginary place for lost, forgotten or unwanted persons or things; an unknown intermediate place or condition between two extremes; a region on the border of hell. *Dead-end* is defined as having no exit, permitting no opportunity for advancement, a position of no hope or progress; a blind alley. Being in limbo or in a dead-end situation breeds confusion because there seems to be no end in sight. It is impossible to plan anything because you do not know how long you will be in this place and you simply do not know what to do.

For the first couple of years of my relationship with the minister, I was okay. I thought that this was a reasonable time frame in which people who loved each other need in order to prepare to be married. The remaining three years of the relationship, felt like a region on the border of hell! I had no hope or progress in this relationship. I felt confined and confused. It felt like I was left alone, forgotten and unwanted in a blind alley. I felt like I was neither here nor there but kind of just sitting there, waiting on this man to get his act together. In reality, all I had to do was make a decision myself to end it, but yet again I did not want to lose all of the time I had spent. I felt like the time I spent should count for something and I wanted a return on my investment. I had to finally suck it up and call it quits when I realized this man could not deliver and for my own sanity, I needed to walk myself out of this limbo before I lost my mind. It is absolutely the most weird, hard place to be sisters. Whatever you do, don't get stuck in limbo land with a man!

Being this state slowly unraveled me over time. By my very nature, I tend to be orderly and like to have closure. I like to move on to do the next thing in life. However, being in this relationship caused me to lose my sense of poise and peace. Not only that, because I was always strung out in underlying anxiety, tension, and nervousness all the time I could not properly focus on walking in my purpose. I spent the bulk of my emotional energy wondering where this confusing relationship was going to go. It was getting more and more difficult for me to justify to myself why I was sitting here in limbo, especially after my father died. I could no longer reconcile what I was seeing with my own eyes, what my spirit was telling me and the feelings I had in my heart. My head, my eyes and the Spirit of Truth kept telling me that this situation was not healthy.

Yet, my heart wanted to keep believing, keep praying, and keep hanging on. Our heart desires are so powerful. This is why God specifically tells us to guard our hearts with *all* diligence for out of it truly comes the issues of life. You simply cannot afford to give your heart away without the guidance of the Holy Spirit and Wisdom. It is just too risky and dangerous. It could literally kill you and your destiny. McKinney Hammond and Brooks state: *"The heart chooses, but the head must qualify the choice. You can feel right about the wrong thing. Listen to your heart, but use your head to sift its information..."* My heart and love for him kept me in the state of confusion because I just didn't want to accept the truth staring me in my face.

Once you have lived in a limbo state in a dead-end relationship, the desire for peace and clarity reigns supreme. Having lived this way myself for way too long, I understand firsthand the pain, the confusion and inner turmoil. This is what I call "faking the funk". This is where you smile and act like everything is okay in front of others when really deep down on the inside you are most miserable. This is where you hate it when people ask questions like, *"When are you two getting married?" or* How come we never see him?" or "What's going on with him?" So you have to come up with some lame-brain reason that you barely believe yourself anymore. Living this way creates internal confusion which is the opposite of the peace that passes all understanding that Christ died to give to us. Girlfriend, no doubt there have times in church where you did what I did – turned to my neighbor to the left and to the right, repeated whatever positive confession the pastor told us to say, gave a big happy smile and hearty handshake and all the while hurting and jacked up! No more living like this!

Another cause of the confusion created in a dead-end relationship is simply the confusing and misleading behavior of the man himself. A man who is not living his life in God's purpose for him and who is not really interested in having a committed relationship with you will create confusion. He will try to keep his options open without having to make a decision to be committed to you. The decision that needs to be made is: *"Do I want to be with you in a committed relationship leading to marriage?"* The answer is "Yes" or "No." If he decides that he doesn't want to marry you, he knows that he will lose the benefit of having you around so he doesn't want to say "No." If he says he is going to commit to you, it means that you will expect him to actually carry through on that commitment, so he doesn't want to say "Yes" either.

Therefore, his best option is to take advantage of your love for him, your strong overriding desire to become married, your emotional attachment and general feminine compassion to keep you in a state of limbo or indecision. He is able to keep you in limbo because of his many and various excuses, reasons and justifications as to why he is not ready to be committed. This is what breeds the painful confusion and chaos for you but for him, it is perfect. It is easier to string you a long with a dangling, perpetually moving carrot than to give an affirmative yes or no. Making a decision and following through with it eliminates confusion. A man who is living his life in God's purpose for him will have integrity in his relationship with you. If he wants to be in your life, he will be fully present and it will be clear. If he does not want to be with you in a committed relationship, he will be honest and will tell you. This brings clarity and not confusion.

Reflect on God's Word

1. 1 Corinthians 14:40 (NKJV) *"Let all things be done decently and in order..."*

2. 1 Corinthians 14:33 (NKJV), *"For God is not the author of confusion, but of peace, as in all churches of the saints."*

3. Romans 8:6 (NIV) *"The mind governed by the flesh is death, but the mind governed by the Spirit is life and peace."*

Things to Think About

1. How peaceful, poised and orderly is your lifestyle? As it is without, so it is within. In other words, if your outward lifestyle is unorganized, all over the place, and you are running from crisis to crisis, chances are this is the way you are on the inside. What are you doing to increase the order in your life? If you have a chaotic life, you are your own worst enemy and are self-sabotaging your own destiny. The kind of man you would like as a husband would see you as a hindrance and not as a helpmeet.

2. Are you in relationship (not just romantic) with someone that always has some type of drama and chaos that touches your life in some way? Are you attracted to the drama and chaos because it is your opportunity to show how you can "help" them and come to their "rescue"? They can always depend on you to come through (even though it wears you out and costs you money and

time). However, you do it because you want to be seen as the "Go-To" person when things get bad. How is this working for you?

3. Often, a dead-end relationship has the added element of extra drama/chaos as well. Should this relationship actually move to commitment or marriage, the drama will not go away. Are you currently in a dead-end relationship and is it causing loss of internal peace and poise for you? Have you counted the cost of being in a dead-end relationship for an indefinite period of time? Time cannot be regained. Once it is gone, you never get it back.

Chapter 8
Whole & Healthy Romance – No More Crumb Snatching

Because I was a broken woman and did not realize I was broken, I attracted another broken individual in my life. Two broken people do not make a whole relationship. What you end up with is a mess! When a whole man and a whole woman come together, they create a healthy and wholesome relationship. A healthy relationship is one in which both individuals are strong and whole before they come together. They have both worked with God to receive healing, to grow up and mature individually so that they both have something to bring to the relationship table. This is not to say that they are both perfect. However, this is to say that they are both actively growing and becoming stronger every day. We are talking about a two individuals that realize their weaknesses, issues and concerns and are actively dealing with their stuff. They are not hiding it, running away from it, or pretending it doesn't exist. We are talking about people that have reached a point in their lives where they have enough confidence in whom they are that they no longer carry the shame of the past on them and are already walking in a certain level of peace, wholeness, and deliverance from their past mistakes.

When two broken people come together, they are both struggling. They cannot complement each other, but rather they are attempting to snatch crumbs from each other while at the same time trying to develop and maintain a relationship. It is very difficult to have the necessary give-and-take because broken people always need to take since they don't have a lot to give. A broken women trying to fix, help, or heal a man is trying to "take" her self-worth and value from fixing the man so she can marry him. A broken man who is spiritually and emotionally unavailable to fully function in the relationship is simply trying to "take" what he needs from the woman in the moment by pretending that he is fully vested in the relationship when he knows full well that he is not.

The end result is both parties attempting to snatch crumbs from each other under the guise of coming together. For example, if a relationship was the equivalent of a whole cake or a whole loaf of bread, than an unhealthy relationship with two crumb snatching individuals would appear to be two broken halves attempting to come together but creating more breakage. A healthy relationship, on the other hand, would resemble two halves actually coming together to make a whole and complete cake with icing on top. In the broken cake, both individuals are snatching crumbs from each other to the detriment of the whole cake.

A Snapshot of the Crumb Snatching Woman

A *crumb* is defined as a very small piece broken from a baked item, such as a cookie, cake or bread. It is also defined as a small fragment, scrap or portion. From this definition, a whole piece or part would be a full portion or a full serving. In terms of a romantic relationship, a crumb could represent the smallest piece or bit that an individual could contribute to a relationship in terms of time, commitment and support. On the other hand, a full serving represents when both individuals freely give to each other the time, commitment and support in order create a vibrant, whole and full romantic relationship.

A woman who is functioning in a relationship from a place of brokenness has no real sense of what wholeness and what normalcy in a relationship looks like. From her perspective, anything received from a man is better than nothing at all. In my case, I went without true emotional and spiritual intimacy for so long in my marriage that I fell for the first Christian man who showed interest. From my perspective at that time, because he was a Christian (and a minister), showed genuine interest and said the right words in the beginning of the relationship, he was "The One".

I was the Queen of Crumbs. Because I was not complete in Christ and the desire for marriage was so strong in my heart, I was willing to accept crumbs in a relationship if it meant that ultimately I would be married. I was also unaware of the fact that because of my willingness to accept crumbs, it meant that I was still not yet ready for the whole and complete relationship that I deeply desired.

Because I had a heart of compassion and could see the potential in a man, I could very easily justify his crumbs as being the best that he could offer (which it really was) and make excuses in my mind why it was okay for me to accept it. I focused on the potential of a what he could be if he kept receiving my love and understanding instead of the reality of who he really was (which is all he was ever going to be) until he decided to change within himself.

I could take old leftover crumbs and make a feast out of it for days! In hindsight, what I thought was normal in relationship, was actually crumbs that I built up to make more than what it really was in order to justify it in my mind. For example, a broken woman can live on text messages from her man. If all he did was send lazy text messages all day long or for several days in a row instead of picking up the phone to have a true conversation with her, she would gladly accept this crumb. If he only drops by at night or on very short notice at the drop of the hat, she is so happy to see him that she doesn't care if it was an inconvenience or stopped her from doing what she needed to do. She gladly accepts this crumb.

If he gives her money or gifts in lieu of spending quality time with her because he is too "busy", she accepts this crumb as well. If he always breaks dates, does not show up or changes plans at the last minute with some lame excuse, she perfectly understands and receives this crumb as well. If he asks her to draft some proposal, a business document, or his resume she will stay up all night getting it done for him. He will send a thank you text and tell her he will be coming to spend time the next day, but then something happens and he does not show up. She accepts this as part of her crumb meal too.

The crumb-snatching woman needs her daily hit to get her crumb meal. She needs the daily texting, the phone calls and being there for him in order to feel good about herself. If something happens that causes a deviation from the norm – i.e., he goes 24 hours or so without texting or calling, she becomes emotionally upset. She may start blowing up his phone text messages and voice mails. She cannot handle not being in communication with this man because it is her lifeline.

She is so ready to love and be loved that she will jump out and catch any and all crumbs that a man will give her and try to make a full meal – a full relationship out of it. These are the things that I did. I was that broken woman. The revelation that was the key to my transformation process was the realization that Jesus Christ gave *all* of himself to make me whole. I received His wholeness when I accepted what He did on the Cross for me. If I received Christ—then I got ALL of Him -- not a little piece, crumb, slice or a fraction. Since Jesus gave me all of Himself and not little crumbs, then how did I look accepting crumbs in a relationship with a man that professed to love me? Does this really reflect the type of relationship that Jesus died to give me? Why did I gladly accept stale crumbs from a man, reject Christ's wholeness and then have the nerve to wonder why I was still emotionally hungry? Imagine me a full grown woman, trying to piece together some crumbs and end pieces of a sandwich in order to get full meal and be satisfied? Well, sister that's exactly what you are doing if you are accepting scraps from a man in an effort to have a relationship! Say Amen to that!

A whole woman, on the other hand, realizes her value and worth as a Daughter of the King and knows that she deserves more than crumbs and leftovers from a man that claims to love her. She desires and requires a full relationship which has God in the middle, quality time, consistency and reliability. She knows that her man is to put her first after God and to support and build her up instead of always taking and never really giving. She realizes that a real relationship grows in true emotional and spiritual intimacy instead of staying shallow and on the surface. Not only that, a whole woman able to quickly discern a man who does not have the spiritual or emotional capacity to have a whole relationship with her. She is complete and whole in Christ and does not want to jeopardize the wholeness that she is now walking in so she has learned to clearly see the signs of the crumb-snatching man.

A Snapshot of the Crumb-Snatching Man

The crumb-snatching man is a different type altogether. This is the man that knows he is not ready for a real relationship and has no intention to be in a real relationship. He may also be unaware of his own brokenness and thinks that he is ready when he is not. Once the woman involved begins to express her desire for commitment or marriage, his entire modus operandi now changes to keep the relationship at a certain, perpetual state where nothing is expected of him other than the crumbs. This could be the type of relationship where it starts off as just "kicking it" or "hanging out". If she begins to demand more than "kicking it" and "hanging" because she has become emotionally attached, he simply pulls away. Because she is broken, she cannot handle it when he pulls away, goes silent, and drops off the side of the world. By doling out the crumbs and withholding time when necessary, he is able to maintain the status quo so that her expectations are kept in line. This may sound cold, but it is true, as I have experienced this first hand. While in the midst of it, I didn't realize it, but as my eyes became opened, I began to see the pattern very distinctly and very clearly. It was as if the blinders were removed from off my eyes.

This type of man is emotionally unavailable or commitment phobic. He may be borderline narcissistic. There is some underlying problem, wound or soul issue that he does not want to deal with or come clean about that keeps him this way. It is easier for him to secure what he wants from a woman without being truly committed to her. In some ways, women in general have contributed to this by making it easy for a man to have female support, companionship and intimacy without true commitment. This type of man is not a true godly man but a man that takes advantage of vulnerable and broken woman who are needy for love. A whole woman would not allow this type of man and would recognize his pattern immediately. Natalie Lue in her book Mr. Unavailable & the Fallback Girl states:

"Doing some simple basic stuff that available people take for granted takes a lot of effort for him - just the mental effort in showing up feels huge. He might remind you that he brought you something, took you out to dinner, stayed the night, has moved in, or has claimed that you're exclusive because he thinks that this is what commitment takes. He doesn't view his capabilities in reality and may see himself operating at as much as 100%. The very deluded may think it goes beyond that. His 100% is not an available person's 100% because he has limited capacity. The more you put up with it, the more you see a limited capacity as full capacity and the crumbs get magically turned into a loaf. Ever seen someone settle? It's because they decide that something is better than nothing, but that something may be very insubstantial. It's like you're saying "Wow! Look at how much of a limited contribution is coming from a limited man!"... The key is to stop overvaluing the crumbs too and making them into a loaf, because if you saw them as crumbs, you'd have left..." (p. 56-57)

The Crumb Snatching Man wants his crumbs too. He may appear to be very confident, cocky or arrogant but he is actually deeply insecure and has a lot of issues. His main crumbs are: (1) sex without marriage, (2) money, services or resources; and (3) an ego or emotional boost when he is feeling less of a man in the form of puffing him up. A whole man wants a full relationship with love, emotional, spiritual and mental intimacy. A whole man wants to serve and support his woman financially and is not going to take away from her. A whole man is secure in who he is and though he is appreciative of the support of his woman, he is fully capable of building himself up in the Lord because he has his own relationship with God.

Just like you cannot create a full and nutritious meal by piecing together a few measly crumbs, you cannot create a real, full and satisfying relationship with crumbs either. If two people are both intent on getting their crumb supply from each other, they are certainly not going to come together in a cohesive fashion to make a whole relationship. They are living off pieces of each other to their own individual detriment thus contributing to long-term brokenness. This is not a real relationship but rather both people are simply using each other. The sad part is that the woman thinks she is in a relationship when she is not. Both have dishonest agendas operating because both are completely unaware of their hidden desires driving their behaviors.

The reason why we will accept crumbs from a man is because we have a scarcity mentality. An abundant mentality is one that dwells in the realm of being whole, complete and full. There is overflow. There is an abundance where there is nothing lacking or broken in your life. The scarcity mentality is one that is in the realm of being broken, fragmented, having a little bit. It is the crumb mentality.

It takes time to develop the abundant mindset but it is absolutely critical to do so because it will enable you to recognize when you are receiving crumbs from a man and when you are receiving the whole, real thing. The woman with the Scarcity or Lack mentality really and truly thinks she is getting a whole relationship with these crumbs. She knows something is missing and is not quite right but she is able to justify in her mind why these crumbs are acceptable right now because she believes that he will change and magically deliver at a whole and full level someday. Natalie Lue states it beautifully: A crumb is a crumb is a crumb. Unless you're an ant, that crumb doesn't look like a loaf. Either get your eyes tested or take off your magnifying rose tinted glasses and get wise about what healthy relationships look like. Oh, and take him off that pedestal you've put him on while you're at it. There's a guy out there that will commit to you (when you're ready to commit) but that's not going to happen if you stick with Mr. Unavailable. – Natalie Lue, *Mr. Unavailable and the Fallback Girl*, 2nd Edition.

Reflect on God's Word

1. Colossians 2:10 (AMP) *"And you are in Him, made full and having come to fullness of life [in Christ you too are filled with the Godhead--- Father, Son and Holy spirit—and reach full spiritual stature]..."*

2. Ephesians 3:19 (GWT) *You will know Christ's love, which goes far beyond any knowledge. I am praying this so that you may be completely filled with God.*

3. 2 Corinthians 9: 8 (NET) *"And God is able to make all grace overflow to you so that because you have enough of everything in every way at all times, you will overflow in every good work."*

Things to Think About

1. Do you see yourself in the snapshot of a Crumb Snatching Woman? As you review your current and past relationships can you see a pattern of taking what a man gives and attempting to make a meal out of it as if is a full and satisfying relationship?

2. The key to positioning yourself to attracting a whole man is to become a whole woman yourself. The best way to become this type of woman is to deliberately take the time to really get to know and receive Christ on a heart level so that you can become full. This means moving beyond a "head" knowledge of who Jesus is, but a "heart" knowledge so that you can be full in your heart thus not needing crumbs from another human to feel whole on the inside. What are you doing to develop your relationship with Christ first?

3. Meditate on 2 Corinthians 9:8. Note what it says about how God is able to make all grace overflow to you so that you will have enough of everything in every way at all times and that you will overflow into every good work. God is not crumby. Our God is a God of Overflow. It takes faith to believe in and receive this Overflow, but it is critical to

have the Overflow in operation in your life. Else wise, you will have a lack mentality that attracts and lives on crumbs.

Part Three: Move On to a New Season and a New You

Chapter 9
Let it Go

This chapter is the most important one of all. I wasted five years of my life in a dead-end relationship by making it an issue of faith and hanging on anyhow until it was so very obvious that he was with other women. I could have avoided this altogether had I actually paid attention to and heeded the red flags. Ladies, do not make hanging on to a bad relationship an issue of faith, claiming that God is going to change him or the situation. It is the height of foolishness to believe that your prayers will change someone else to suit your agenda which is to be married. God is not obligated to change, move or do anything with these types of underlying motives operating. As long as this is going on, you are making yourself emotionally and spiritually unavailable for the true man God has for you and you are walking in self-deception. In *What Women Don't Know and Men Don't Tell You*, McKinney Hammond & Brooks state:

"...Christian women are famous for making a horrible mistake over and over again: They feel that God has spoken to them about a specific man. We are not saying that God will never speak to your heart about the man you are to marry, but we are saying that it is very dangerous for a woman to get hung up on a feeling. Especially if you see no concrete indication from the other person...We want to help you guard against illusion. When you commit to a man based upon what you believe is a "word from the Lord" you will give him unqualified commitment and consider anything that speaks to the contrary as a test of your faith..."

My question is why did I resist the truth for so long? I had the gift of mercy. I willingly took on his burdens when I had enough of my own and he pretended to be concerned about mine, but he cared more about himself. I was very naïve but he was not. He knew exactly what the real deal was. However, I wanted to hang on to the belief of what I had been praying and expecting God to do instead of seeing the truth -- he lacked integrity and had no intention of marrying me. I kept waiting for God to move on him after I saw clearly the mess I was in. I spent time repenting for both myself and him, but with no clear results. Instead, he seemed to get worse. I was reaping results of self-inflicted isolation, loneliness, emotional numbness along with a good dose of embarrassment and shame. I kept hanging on to the dream first I had in beginning of relationship when everything was hopeful along with the few good things that I received and the few times he was there for me that truly meant something. In, *Mr. Unavailable and the Fallback Girl*, Natalie Lue states:

"A person isn't just about the beginning of the relationship and in actual fact; they're not just about the good times, so you need to see them as a whole and the relationship in context. I've had women ask me why he can't go back to the guy he was at the beginning when they've been with him for eight years and struggling for 7.5 of them! You do the math on that one! You need more than 'good times' and 'moments' to justify sticking in a relationship that's been consistently struggling for longer than it's been consistently good."

I Don't Want to Let Go… I've Put So Much into This Relationship

In addition, I had fallen prey to the idea that he will instantaneously materialize into the wonderful godly man that I knew he was deep on the inside the minute I would break it off. I worried that some other lucky woman will get all the benefit of the investment that I put into him.

I kept hanging on because I had made a profound emotional investment in someone who is not really invested in me. How many of us women have made a huge investment in the life of a man but not the same level of investment in ourselves, our purpose or our own children? What if all of that emotional energy and thinking was spent on you, your children, your dream, and your purpose? Yet, we spend so much time agonizing, obsessing, re-hashing, re-thinking, re-playing conversations, dates, telephone calls over and over again in our minds.

We pour over every text message to analyze it in detail. We think that somehow or another we are going to have some big "Aha" moment of revelation where it all makes sense and we have another reason to justify giving this dead-end, weird, limbo relationship a "little more time to see where it goes." We know where it goes, sisters -- absolutely nowhere but another blind alley! Even though we may see that the situation is not ever going to go anywhere, having the courage to call it quits is still an admission of defeat and is difficult to endure.

I Don't Want to Let Go…. Calling it Quits Means I was Wrong

Pride is also a key factor in staying in a relationship past its expiration date. We are too proud to admit that we were wrong. We do not want to admit that maybe we didn't really hear from God, but rather from our own emotions, hormones, unmet needs, desires and brokenness. We don't want anyone to know the real deal. But the reality is that everyone can see the situation. You are not fooling anyone.

When my father died, it was the last and final straw for me. I did not have the emotional or spiritual capacity to keep going in the same old circles another year. Something had to end. I had finally come to the place of complete surrender. I had made it up in my mind that if the only way that I could finally have some complete peace and quiet in my soul – no more anxiety, no more wondering, figuring, guessing, hoping, praying, and on and on about this relationship was to end it, then so be it. So for the six months prior to working up the nerve to actually end it, I spent an unusual amount of time in prayer. I asked God to open my eyes and specifically prayed to not let me be deceived and to see the truth and to help me accept it.

God always answers prayers that line up with his will! When I began surrendering and giving up my fantasy and asking God to open my eyes, He began to move. This is a real place ladies. This is where it got real so that I could heal! The first signs were I began to become even more perceptive when I could actually tell when he was lying. The more time I spent with God, the more I could discern the lying spirit. God really began to show me some things. I just waited until I was ready and when the moment came, after another instance of confirmation, I knew it was the right time. Shortly after I ended our relationship, even more confirmation came in that let me know that, yes I heard from God, yes the discernment I was operating in was true and yes indeed, I had the courage to let it go. Even when I knew I was ready to let it go, my pride still hurt because I thought I was the exceptional woman that could handle him and help him.

I Don't Want to Let Go....I thought I was The Exception

We are all exceptional and special to God. Each of one of us is unique, fearfully and wonderfully made. There is no one else on earth like you. However, you are not the exception when it comes to the basic nature of men and relationships. This is an incredibly tough and hard pill to swallow. It hurts our feelings to think that we cannot be a powerful, profound influence on a man such that he will come running to us on bended knee about how right and good we are, and he is ready to commit and change for us. Sure, there are cases and exceptions where this has happened. But the reality is that it is quite rare. We want to take the hard, rocky road of fixing, healing and changing someone instead of simply holding out for the one who is already whole and ready to be in a relationship. Why do we always want that hard, jacked up road? Why is it so hard to wait for someone who is right and ready? It is because we believe that we are the exception and that we can handle it. It is because we are impatient and cannot wait so we will take a man and think that "he just needs a little work." No matter how you slice it or add it up, no one woman can change a man. The man must have the basic character already in place and be emotionally and spiritually available for a healthy relationship for you to have a healthy one with him. If he does not have it in place, no matter how wonderful you are, you are not the exception that will cause him to change.

A man has to use his own free will to change. God created him this way. If God does not override a man's free will choice to receive salvation, what makes us think that we can override a man's free will choice to get change for the better and marry us? He has to love you and want you bad enough to pay the price of marriage. If a man does change, it is because *he wanted to change on his own*. It is not because of a woman, even though she may have influence. It is not because of your loving-kindness, busting your boundaries, nagging, helping and fixing. We want to be the exceptional woman that can take an unhealthy, malfunctioning man or a man who simply is not serious about us and create the healthy relationship we envision. We want to live out that image in our heads of how this man could potentially be and what this relationship could potentially become. The problem with this is again it goes back to self-deception. You absolutely cannot afford to live in potential for an indefinite period of time without reality soon catching up.

The tension between what could be (potential) and what really is (reality) is what creates the turmoil, the confusion and the angst. It is what causes the pain and suffering. It is the ultimate pre-cursor to being in a dead-end relationship situation. The pain of this is further exacerbated by the fantasies and imaginations that we have because we really want our reality to line up with the fantasy that we have built up in our heads. On top of that, some Christian women again make it an issue of faith and think that they are "calling those things that be not as though they were" or that they are praying and "speaking the Word" into their situation to change their man. They fail to realize that the man has a free will choice to be who he is no matter how wonderful she is. Natalie Lue goes on to state: *"This is an inverted ego issue - you think you can change someone's fundamental emotional style, values, characteristics, etc. That's a big ask, even for God himself..."* (p.259)

The best way to prove that you are the exceptional woman is to fully live your life and be the best woman you can be for the glory of God. This is what will make you a truly exceptional woman. Many women do not do this. They stay bogged down in their past. They stay bogged down in their emotions. They refuse to rise up and leave the excuses behind in order to become exceptional. Just by being the best you, you will stand out already from the pack of women that are always proving herself, chasing, and fixing a man. You become exceptional by simply being the best you. The first step in becoming an exceptional woman is to shake this relationship off and pick up those God-given dreams again.

Shake the Dust Off Your Feet and Off Your Dreams

The two scriptures below are powerful statements about when it is time for us to shake off some stuff and get free:

"And whosoever shall not receive you, nor hear your words, when ye depart out of that house or city, shake off the dust of your feet..." - Matthew 10:14 (KJV)

"Shake off your dust; rise up, sit enthroned, Jerusalem. Free yourself from the chains on your neck, Daughter Zion..." – Isaiah 52:2 (NIV)

When we prepare to exit the dead-end relationship, we must shake the dust off. Dust can be described as particles of dirt, grime, filth, smut and soot. We cannot afford to walk around with the grime and the soot that accumulated in our souls while sitting in a dead-end relationship. Just like Matthew 10:14 states, it is obvious that the man you were in a relationship with did not really hear your heart cry. He did not really receive you. It is time to depart the "house or city" of this "relationship" and shake off the dust before you walk into your new season. You must be clean and free from the effects of the dead-end relationship before you can rightly walk into your new season. Any soot and grime still lingering on your soul will hinder you as you move forward. It will also prevent a whole relationship with a healthy man with from showing up as well. Christ is the one who specializes in the clean-up process. He is well able to clean you up and prepare you for what is next. Seek Him first.

Not only must we shake the residue of that dead-end situation off of us, we must now return to the dreams and visions that God planted inside of us. As indicated in Isaiah 52:2, we must shake the dust off and return to our rightful place by rising up and getting back on our thrones as the women of God we are called to be. Shake the dust off that business idea. Shake the dust off that book that you have half-written. Shake the dust off those desires and things that you have been intending to do, but put on hold because you were "waiting" on that man to get his act together so that you could finally get married.

Reflect on God's Word

1. Philippians 3:13 (AMP) *"I do not consider, brethren, that I have captured and made it my own [yet]; but one thing I do [it is my one aspiration]: forgetting what lies behind and straining forward to what lies ahead."*

2. Isaiah 43:18-19 (MSG) *"Forget about what's happened; don't keep going over old history. Be alert, be present. I'm about to do something brand-new..."*

3. 2 Corinthians 5:17 (AMP) *"Therefore if any person is [ingrafted] in Christ (the Messiah) he is a new creation (a new creature altogether); the old [previous moral and spiritual condition] has passed away. Behold, the fresh and new has come."*

Things to Think About

1. As you honestly consider your current situation, is it possible that you have made staying in this relationship an issue of faith? Do you believe that you have heard from God and that this relationship is God's will for you, but somehow the man just doesn't quite get it yet?

If you believe that this man is your God-ordained husband, wouldn't it be reassuring to know that he actually hears and obeys God if you plan to follow him as he follows Christ? With that said, how come your future husband still hasn't heard what you are hearing from God after all of this time?

2. It is fear that keeps us bound and stuck in limbo. Fear of admitting that we were just flat out wrong about this man. Fear that we have made a big, huge mistake. Fear of what people will think of us after all the time we spent in this relationship. Fear that we will be alone forever. No matter how disheartening and painful the hard, cold reality of the situation is that truth is healthier and is better for you in the long-run. We cannot live a relationship lie and expect God's blessings. The mess, the fantasy, the hoping and the wishing feels good but it is hurting you more than you know. God has not given to us a spirit of fear but of power love and a sound mind. The truth is what ultimately sets us free. Write down your fears that keep you bound in this relationship. Write down the reasons why you keep hanging on.

3. Being honest with yourself and surrendering to God is the first step. The next step is to actually let go the past and move forward. This is easier said than done. God is ready to up us move forward, heal us and re-build our lives, but first we must make a non-negotiable decision to let the façade of this relationship go and move forward. He can make all things new and is able to do an entirely new thing in your life if you let Him. Are you really tired of this mess and ready to move forward?

Chapter 10
Rebuilding Your New Life

After much prayer and struggle, you finally have the courage to leave the dead-end relationship. Once you end the relationship, you must be prepared to deal with the onslaught of emotions, thoughts, and revelations that are sure to come. Now that it is over, you will begin to see even more clearly how sad the situation really was.

When you make the choice to leave and actually follow through with it, everything all of a sudden becomes crystal clear. There is no more limbo. There is no confusion. There is an immediate sense of peace that comes when you have finally made a decision that actually benefits and increases you as a woman. However, with all of that, there is emotional pain and thoughts that need to be processed and worked through. That is what the shaking the dust off process is about. It is about dealing with the emotions that come up. It is about healing from the emotional wounds that being in dead-end situation created. It is really about walking with God to bring restoration to all areas of your life so that you can enter your next season with wholeness, peace and clarity.

Without taking the time to process, work through and deal with these emotions and revelations, you could be immediately drawn right back into another dead-end relationship. The pain of processing seems to be too much to bear. It's much easier to avoid dealing with it by diving right back into full-on dating and being busy with other distractions than to deal with your feelings and heart issues. In reality, once you face that pain and walk through it, it is better for you in the long run. The pain of coming to grips of where you are and how you got here will end the faster you face it. On the other side of healthy, healing pain is victory and peace. On the other side of unhealthy, staying stuck pain is even greater emotional and spiritual damage. In fact, the damage extends beyond you to the people around you at this point. Not only that, the pain of limbo affects the people you were supposed to touch had you moved on and did what God told you to do, instead of waiting around in that relationship. As you begin to process the relationship, many questions will come to mind that need to be answered.

Why Did I Stay in This Relationship So Long?

The question of the day as you began to process and unravel why it took you so long to finally leave this mess is: *"Why in the world did I put myself through all of this to start with? How come I ignored the signs, the warnings, the red flags, etc.? Why did take me so long to get a clue?"* Then you start to get angry with yourself about how you wasted your time for so long. You may feel upset with yourself when you realize that everyone around you knew the real deal and here you are just now coming to grips with it.

On some level, you needed this experience in order to learn the lesson you needed to learn. On some level, you attracted an unhealthy situation in your life. God allowed it for specific and strategic reasons that were crucial to your growth and development as a woman. God does not waste anything and all things truly work together for good (Romans 8:28). Also, there is the plain and simple fact that you are a human being who sins and who lives in a sinful world. That is why Jesus came to start with. Because of the original sin of Adam and Eve, the world as we know it is forever functioning under the shadow and stain of darkness, sin, sickness, accidents, death and sorrow. Because we live in this world, we will make bad choices and suffer. Other people will make bad choices and we will suffer. The good, the bad, the ugly, the Christians and the non-Christians – we will all suffer in some way, shape form or fashion.

The difference between a Christian who suffers and the non-Christian who suffers is the redemptive hope and power of Christ, the Ultimate Sufferer at work in the Christian's life.

What Should I Do During this Healing Season?

The primary issue of the healing from the dead-end relationship that creates problems for us is the natural tendency as humans to run away from God instead of running to him. When we suffer, instead of drawing closer to Christ, we run from him, thus intensifying and delaying our own healing process – in essence, cutting our noses off in spite of our face.

The reason why we tend to shy away from the things of God during the suffering season is because we question God and His love for us because of our pain. We fail to understand how a loving God that we have served would allow this to happen to us. How could God allow me to stay in this situation? How come he did not reveal this to me earlier? Why couldn't I see it? The focus is on our pain and suffering and not on God and who He is. It is also an element of pride involved. We don't like the fact that we "missed" God's timing or will in this whole entire relationship situation and we feel like we should've known better. He can take your arguments, your anger and your whys. He simply waits for you to come to him and continually draws you to Himself. Essentially, the key to the healing, is no matter how bad you feel is to continue to pray, continue to go to church, continue to read your Bible, continue to fellowship with other believers, especially those who you can trust.

Somehow through the grace and mercy of God, you eventually come to yourself, wake up and smell the coffee, so to speak and you look at your life and some semblance of light begins to appear. You start feeling a bit better and you begin to assess your true situation. However, instead of getting happy because you are feeling better, you begin to really see the effects of what happened to you. You see your surroundings and your lifestyle with more clarity.

This doesn't mean victory is imminent. Often during this season, you may take several downward slips. Often you must go down again and again before you can go up. Why is this so? It is because reality is setting in. You see how much emotional, mental, spiritual and natural work that it is going to take to be whole again -- to be normal again. You see the mistakes you made. You have regrets. The old issues from the past are still there.

During this season of assessing your situation, there are several keys to help you navigate through this process:

- **Realize that you are human.** You will make mistakes. You are not perfect. That's why you need God every single day of your life.

- **Receive God's grace.** Just like you got saved by grace, you will be sanctified by grace, healed by grace and your life re-built by grace – not by your brain power, schemes, plans in the flesh. Stop using the world's standards as a measure of your life and look at your life through God's eyes. Ask for the mind of Christ

- **Take care of yourself.** Have people you can trust in your life. Learn to trust again.

- **Learn in the process**. Learn what works and doesn't work. Be humble.

- **Forgive yourself, those you hurt you and forgive God**. Yes! I said forgive God. You have been walking around mad, angry and resentful toward God because He allowed certain things. Although your experiences may not have all been great, they served in making up the quality of woman you are today. For that alone I'm sure you can agree it was all worth it!

Now that you are leaning all the way into your healing process, you are not running away from God. You are not getting busy and distracted to avoid being alone with your pain. You are spending quality time with God to replenish and build up your soul. You are working through forgiving the man for the pain he caused and forgiving yourself for permitting this situation in your life. You are coming to grips with and owning your mess and taking responsibility for your life and your choices. What does it really take to shake the dust off, rebuild and restore your life? In order to do this you must first assess where you right now.

Survey the Ruins

To survey something means to look at something carefully and thoroughly so as to appraise it. It also means to examine or record the area and features of land so as to construct a map, plan or description. For you to begin the process of re-building your life and getting back on track after having been in a dead-end relationship for so long, you must take the time to look at your life very carefully. You must examine all areas of your life to see exactly how being in this relationship has affected you and what you must do next. This is the perfect time to really make a conscious choice on how you want your life to look and what you want to accomplish.

It is an opportunity for you to deliberately design your life according to your terms --- the terms that God has placed in your heart for you to accomplish. No more reactionary, default style living. You are now in a position where you can live your life by design and on purpose, not based on following a man who does not really know where he is going, waiting on a man for marriage, or reacting to and responding to his crises or chaos. You can now live for you! Surveying the ruins is no quick work. It can be quite painful as you come to some realizations and see the areas where you got off track and fell off the wagon during the time you spent in this relationship. You will be able to clearly see things in your life that you placed on the back burner that should be in full operation at this point but you lost momentum when you got caught up in the relationship.

Speaking for myself, as I began to survey the ruins and review what this relationship cost me, it became very painful. It was difficult to see what had happened in my life as the blinders were removed and the relationship was over. I now had to face the reality which was in my face all along. I saw how it affected my self-esteem and impacted my ability to trust. Because of being strung out in that relationship for so long, I had anxiety issues which caused digestive troubles. I had suffered emotional wounds due to the loneliness, embarrassment and the pain caused by his lack of integrity. My parenting was impacted because I saw that I spent more time praying for him, his stuff and my own agenda than my children. When I woke up and smelled the coffee, I realized that I now had a teenager on my hands who was beginning to display issues. My financial situation was also impacted negatively. I was not fully functioning in the gifts and talents God had given me to serve in my local church because I was too busy using my talents to help him. I had delayed my destiny and purpose in God.

Clean up the Ruins

Now that you have made an assessment of how this relationship has impacted your life, you must begin the process of cleaning up and re-building. Again, this is no quick work. It took you years to get to this point in life, and it will take more than two days or two weeks to clean up and re-build your life. The longer the time you spent in the dead-end situation, the longer it will take to get your life back on track. However, as you work with God, he can accelerate your clean-up process as you work with Him. If you try to do it in your own power, you will fail.

The clean-up process itself begins with very practical and wise decisions. It is not all spiritual and emotional. You must make quality, practical decisions to get your life together. You must be willing to take responsibility, work and not run from it. My ruin clean-up process actually began before I officially ended the relationship. I already had my foot half-way out the door, because I my eyes were already opened up to what was going on, I just didn't quite have the courage to leave right then. But I had already began attending a new church. I started giving my tithes as well as serving. This immediately increased my peace level.

As I began to saturate in the Word that was preached, my confidence and courage grew. I was beginning to get healed on the inside and began to have hope for the first time in a very long time. Shortly after the break-up, I decided that I would pick back up with my writing and I started a blog. This represented another increase in confidence that I was heading in the right direction and God's hand was upon my life for good in spite of the mess and the mistakes. When the time came to go to new member's class and join the church, I didn't waste any time. One thing that I learned from being in a dead-end situation, is that time is absolutely non-renewable. Once that time is gone in your life, you cannot get it back. I made a decision that I was not going to waste any more time in my life on fruitless, non-productive relationships and activities. From this point on, if a relationship or activity did not produce or have value for my life, the lives of my children or God's work than I would not be doing it. I quickly got plugged into a ladies life/bible study group at my church. I spent too much time in isolation and decided that I needed the accountability, healing and friendship that the group offered. No more struggling by myself!

I put my children into a mentoring program and began to study about parenting. I focused on my home environment and ways to become a better mother. I began to research and study on different things that I could do from a business and ministry perspective in order to increase and elevate my life so that I could quickly get back on track. All of the energy I poured into that relationship, I began to pour into myself and my children. It is not easy and is still an ongoing process.

As you look at your life, think about the steps you need to take that will bring an immediate increase in your peace and confidence. The basic steps I took had simple, yet profound impact on my confidence and willingness to do other things to improve my life. All it takes is a few simple steps. Once you take one step, the other steps to take will quickly manifest. Do not allow fear of what other people will think or what could potentially happen next hinder you from cleaning up your ruins by making quality, practical decisions. Just taking preliminary baby steps will be enough to get you going. You absolutely cannot afford to waste any more time in your life.

In the Power in Waiting, Carla Cannon poses a serious question: *"How long are you going to waste time and not do what the Lord has called you to do? You have a purpose, God has a plan, and He wants to reveal it to you if you would sit still long enough for Him to talk to you. For some of you reading this, God has already given you clear instructions and you are either allowing the opinions of others or your own personal opinions of yourself hinder you..."*

Once you have taken practical steps, you still must deal with the inner emotional stuff that is going on. The cleaning up process is necessary to get to a true foundation so that you can build from new. The old must be cleared away because your new life cannot be built upon the rubbish and residue of the past. The practical, outside steps are the crucial and necessary beginnings to get you in the proper framework, but you still must do the inner work as well. The inner work that takes place during this season involves being able to forgive him and not allow your emotions to get back involved again. There are common pitfalls that you must avoid as you begin to rebuild your life.

The "I-bet-He-regrets-losing-me-now" Syndrome

During this time of getting your life back on track, you will think of him. You may miss him. You will wonder how he is doing. You will remember certain dates or milestones as they roll around in the months ahead. Certain events, things, or activities will trigger a memory. It is impossible to go through life without something reminding you of him or the relationship. As things happen to trigger the memories or the thoughts, inevitably you will begin to wonder if he is thinking of you the way you are thinking of him. You will wonder if he regrets losing you. You may secretly hope that he all of a sudden reaches out to you with deep heartfelt apologies for how badly he treated you, and share how much he misses you, how things are going to be different and how he will marry you instantly. You want him to say all of the things you wished he said while you were together.

Or you may hope that he is suffering with deep remorse and sadness over how he behaved. You may hope that he is with some other woman that is less than half the woman you are and now he really sees what he lost. You think, *"I bet he misses the water now that his well has run dry."* You want him to suffer and feel some pain for all of the pain and confusion he caused by stringing you along with empty promises, crumbs and chaos.

The problem with this line of thinking is that it may feel good for a little while, but it has the net effect of putting mental and emotional energy back into the past when that same energy really needs to be directed to your present and rebuilding your life. Secondly, the desire for him to suffer is really a desire for revenge or to get back to him. You may never actually carry out a plan or a scheme to "get him back," but to harbor the thoughts carries the same weight and has the same effect on your spirit. In Romans 12:19, we read that *"Vengeance is mine, saith the Lord, I will repay..."*

It helps to realize that although his actions or his sin affected you profoundly and deeply, that ultimately his sin was against God. He did it to God, not you. Therefore, the recompense belongs to God. It is in God's hands to handle and not yours. In Galatians 6:7, it states: *"Do not be deceived: God cannot be mocked. A man reaps what he sows..."* He will reap a painful harvest for the actions that he has done that hurt you. You need not worry about how it will happen. You need not waste precious mental and spiritual energy on speculating as to the particulars of his harvest season. God may or may not allow you to see it or hear of it. At any rate, just know in your heart that it is God's issue to handle and not yours. Your job is to focus on getting your life together and not waste time hoping that God hurries up and punishes him for what he did.

Your job is to hold your peace, hold your head up high and hold on to your dreams. Your job is to let go of the past, let go of the bitterness and let go of the pain. Your job during this season as you take the practical steps for restoration and rebuilding is to learn to forgive him and live again.

But I Really Don't Feel Like Forgiving Him

For you to move forward and to be free and clear for a healthy, whole relationship, you must forgive him. Otherwise, you will remain broken and attract another dead-end, limbo relationship. You will attract another emotionally and spiritually unavailable man because harboring unforgiveness in your heart makes you emotionally and spiritually unavailable. For the sake of your own sanity and emotional health, you must forgive him. It is a choice and a decision, not a feeling. Do not allow your feelings to keep you from making the decision to forgive. Your feelings will catch up later. The best way to forgive is to make an effort to pray for him. Praying for him is the last thing on earth you want to do, but it helps facilitate your freedom and ability to forgive. It is difficult to harbor ill feelings towards someone if you are praying for them. Since you already know that he has a harvest coming based on how he treated you, you can pray that God will have mercy upon him, open his eyes and bring repentance before it is too late. This is the best way to speed up your emotional recovery process. It is about you getting to where you need to be, not about him getting away with anything.

He Had the Audacity to Call/Text/Reach Out To Me!

After a period of no contact, he may put his "feelers" out there to see if he can evoke some type of response from you. He may express remorse over losing you. He may express sorrow and say a lot of sweet words of reconciliation. If you have not done the work in the previous chapters, you could fall back into the mess all over again.

Do not be deceived into thinking that he has spontaneously combusted into Mr. Perfect and is all of a sudden now ready for a full, whole and committed relationship. Remember, the same issues that caused you to ultimately leave were never resolved and they are not resolved now if he is the same person. However, if you have worked through your issues you are a different woman now.

You have a greater sense of internal wholeness, completeness and peace. You do not desire the chaos, drama, and the emotional ups and downs anymore. You have experienced a new level of emotional freedom and are well in the process of rebuilding your life. You have no desire leave your seated position as a Daughter of the King to go back down to the same mess again.

As a whole woman, you will see his attempt to reach out to you for what it is --- he is not really interested in a true relationship and he hasn't really changed. He just wants his crumbs back and you were a very easy supply back when you were broken and thought that crumbs were a real relationship. With the grace of God, you have forgiven him, but at this point he no longer has access to the inner circle of your life anymore. He is an acquaintance that you know from afar. You are now very careful about who you allow close to because you now walk in wisdom by the Spirit and not by your emotions.

Reflect on God's Word

1. **Survey the Ruins** - Nehemiah 2: 13, 17 (NIV): *"By night I went out through the Valley Gate toward the Jackal[a] Well and the Dung Gate, examining the walls of Jerusalem, which had been broken down, and its gates, which had been destroyed by fire. Then I said to them, "You see the trouble we are in: Jerusalem lies in ruins, and its gates have been burned with fire. Come, let us rebuild the wall of Jerusalem, and we will no longer be in disgrace."*

2. **Clean Up the Ruins** – Nehemiah 4: 10 (AMP) – *"And [the leaders of] Judah said, the strength of the burden bearers is weakening, and there is much rubbish; we are not able to work on the wall."*

Things to Think About

1. Read the first four chapters of Nehemiah. Nehemiah faced the huge task of rebuilding the walls of the city of Jerusalem. It was in ruins and there was a lot of rubbish. It required great leadership and organization plus the people had to be willing to work. On top of that, he faced opposition and distraction from haters who didn't want to see Jerusalem rise again.

2. As you begin to survey the ruins in your life, what are some immediate steps you can take right now to start the process? Who do you need in your life that can help you?

3. How are you going to handle the pitfalls and distractions that will keep you stuck? Don't let the magnitude of the situation overwhelm you and you wind up not doing anything but sitting in the ruins.

The End - A New Journey

It requires a great deal of strength and energy to clean up ruins that have been wasted for a length of time. As you come to grips with the reality of your life without the relationship and get accustomed to your new status, you may become weary. The weariness comes into play when you realize that you must make a conscious effort to re-direct all of that mental, emotional and spiritual energy back into your life and your purpose that was previously entangled up in the dead-end relationship. This requires effort and takes time. Pace yourself by taking baby steps each day to renew your mind and gather strength from God through bible study and prayer. Remember, your life did not get this way overnight and it will take some time to clean it up. In Galatians 6:9 we are reminded to *"not be weary in well doing: for in due season we shall reap if we faint not."*

As you embark on your new journey of wholeness remember that in order to redeem the time spent in the dead-end relationship, you must become a wise steward of the time you have right now and start moving forward right now. Time is always in forward motion. Time does not stand still or go backwards. God can't redeem anything if you are standing still and do not move forward in a position to receive. While you are waiting be encouraged and remember: Our God is a performing and perfecting God. He performs all things for us (Ps 57:1 NKJV). He perfects the things that concern us (Ps. 138:8). All things are possible with him. (Matt 19:26 NKJV). Every step of preparation, getting ready and getting clear will position you for accelerated restoration.

One key thing to remember as you begin to heal and reflect on the relationship you will notice that not all has been wasted. You learned things about yourself and God that you would have never known otherwise if you had not been in those particular situations. There are nuggets of wisdom and experiences that you now have that can be utilized to help position and prepare you for walking in your purpose. Take all of the learning, pain and experiences and put it to good use by helping someone else in their struggle. Use the experience as a stepping stone to catapult you into your next season. Your testimony of overcoming and walking through to the other side is exactly what someone else needs to hear!

Appendix

Prayer of Salvation

Lord Jesus, I need you in my life. I realize how far I am from you and I see the effects and consequences of my sin. I confess my sins to you and ask for your forgiveness. I ask that you come into my heart as my Lord and Savior. Thank you for eternal life and forgiveness of my sins. Help me to follow you and grow in you forever. I give my life to you. Make me and mold me into the woman of God that you would have me to be.

In Jesus' Name I pray,

Amen.

Prayer for Healing & Deliverance from a Dead-End Relationship

Lord Jesus,

I come before you realizing how this relationship has kept me in bondage. I realize that my life is not bringing you true glory because of being in a relationship that has not been ordained by you. I confess my sin of not trusting in you. I allowed my emotions and my own agenda for getting married or to be in a relationship dominate my life. I confess that I have been unwilling to wait on your timing for the right relationship and I have been unavailable to receive your best in my life because I chose to entangle myself in this relationship for all of the wrong reasons. Help me to face the truth and give me the courage and the grace to let it go.

I ask that you forgive me. Help me to forgive myself. I ask for your cleansing power to come in and set me free. Enable and empower me to break free from the cycle of destructive relationships that do not bring you glory and that stop me from developing into the purpose that You created me for. Help me to become rooted, grounded, fixed and founded in your love. Help me to fully walk in the completeness and wholeness that you died for me to have. Let me walk free with a clean slate and no condemnation for my past relationship mistakes. From this day forward, I now walk into my newly restored life a true Daughter of the King and I sit your courts as a full, free and favored Woman of God.

In Jesus' Name I pray,

Amen.

Endnotes

Chapter 1

Fixed. 2013. In thefreedictionary.com. Retrieved June 1, 2013 from http://www.thefreedictionary.com/fixed

Chapter 2

Wikipedia, The Free Encyclopedia.
http://en.wikipedia.org/wiki/Personal_boundaries Accessed June 12, 2013

Mandy Hale, http://thesinglewoman.net/2013/03/31/the-importance-of-boundaries/ The Importance of Boundaries, March 31, 2013 accessed June 12, 2013.

Michelle McKinney Hammond & Joel A. Brooks, Jr. What Woman Don't Know (And Men Don't Tell You) The unspoken Rules of Finding Lasting Love. WaterBrook Press 2009 or 2011 (pp. 43-45)

Dr. Henry Cloud, John Townsend Boundaries: When to Say Yes, How to Say No to Take Control of Your Life, Zondervan, 1992 Grand Rapids Michigan

Chapter 3

Settle It In Your Soul: YOU Have Been Made Whole. Tonika Maria Breeden, Lady TB LadiesLovingGod Blog www.ladieslovinggodwordpress.com, May 5, 2013, accessed August 15 2013.

Strong's Concordance 7965www.biblehub.com Accessed 1/28/14. http://biblehub.com/hebrew/7965.htm

Chapter 4

Michelle McKinney Hammond & Joel A. Brooks, Jr. What Woman Don't Know (And Men Don't Tell You) The unspoken Rules of Finding Lasting Love. WaterBrook Press 2009 or 2011 (p.122)

Carla R. Cannon. The Power in Waiting: What Do You Do When What God Said Doesn't Line Up With What You Currently See? Carla Cannon. 2013

Chapter 5

Sophia A. Nelson. Black Woman Redefined: Dispelling Myths and Discovering Fulfillment in the Age of Michelle Obama 2012. BenBella Books, Inc. Dallas, TX pp. 244 and 248.

Jackie Kendall & Debby Jones Lady In Waiting: Becoming God's Best While Waiting For Mr. Right.2012. Destiny Image Publishers, Inc. Shippensburg, PA pp. 114, 113

When You Honor Yourself You Honor God. Tonika Maria Breeden, Lady TB LadiesLovingGod Blog www.ladieslovinggodwordpress.com, February 18, 2013, accessed August 15 2013

Chapter 6

Michelle McKinney Hammond & Joel A. Brooks, Jr. What Woman Don't Know (And Men Don't Tell You) The unspoken Rules of Finding Lasting Love. WaterBrook Press 2009 or 2011 (p.37)

Chapter 7

Eunice Leong-Tan. Secrets of Elegance: How to Become Elegant Step by Step. 2010. Lulu.com Raleigh, NC p. 35

Michelle McKinney Hammond & Joel A. Brooks, Jr. What Woman Don't Know (And Men Don't Tell You) The unspoken Rules of Finding Lasting Love. WaterBrook Press 2009 or 2011 (p.11)

Chapter 8

Natalie Lue. Mr. Unavailable and the Fallback Girl. 2010 2nd edition Published by Naughty Girl Media UK

When You Honor Yourself You Honor God. Tonika Maria Breeden, Lady TB, LadiesLovingGod Blog www.ladieslovinggodwordpress.com, February 18, 2013, accessed August 15 2013

Chapter 9

Michelle McKinney Hammond & Joel A. Brooks, Jr. What Woman Don't Know (And Men Don't Tell You) The unspoken Rules of Finding Lasting Love. WaterBrook Press 2009 or 2011 (p.11)

Natalie Lue. Mr. Unavailable and the Fallback Girl 2010 2nd edition Published by Naughty Girl Media. UK

Chapter 10

Settle It In Your Soul: YOU Have Been Made Whole. Tonika Maria Breeden, Lady TB, LadiesLovingGod Blog www.ladieslovinggodwordpress.com, February 18, 2013, accessed August 15 2013

No Condemnation No Separation. Tonika Maria Breeden, Lady TB, LadiesLovingGod Blog www.ladieslovinggodwordpress.com, written August 2013, published, April 5, 2014.

Carla R. Cannon. The Power in Waiting: What Do You Do When What God Said Doesn't Line Up With What You Currently See? Carla Cannon. 2013

All Definitions of words are taken from either www.thefreeonlinedictionary.com or www.merriam-webster.com.

Acknowledgments

I am very thankful and grateful to my mother, Linda Johnson Tillman, a great source of strength, wisdom and love in my life.

To my sister, Myra Denise Thomas, and best friend since high school, Cassandra Adams Hall, for your love, support, and understanding through the years – the many laughs and various tears.

I also wish to acknowledge all of the ladies of the Emerge Life Group, past and present at new**hope** church under Dr. Benji W. Kelley for their love and support as I transitioned out of a dead-end relationship and moved on to my new life.

Lastly, I thank God for my two boys, Michael and Trey, who were always in my corner while writing this book. I love you guys.

About The Author

Tonika M. Breeden is an author and the mother of two boys in Durham, North Carolina. She is actively involved and serving God at her local church as a women's life group leader. After enduring various relationship struggles by learning how to walk complete in Christ, her passion is to help other women navigate tough relationship issues with completeness, clarity and wholeness in Christ. She firmly believes that a woman must become rooted, grounded, fixed and founded in the love of God *first* before being ready for a Christ-centered marriage.

Get Connected!

Connect with Tonika via her website, Facebook or Twitter at:

www.tonikabreeden.com
Twitter: @GetRealBeHealed
Facebook: www.facebook.com/getrealbehealed

39889485R00073

Made in the USA
Lexington, KY
16 March 2015